Penguin Education
Penguin Science of Behaviour
General Editor: B. M. Foss

Social Psychology
Editor: Michael Argyle

Teachers and Teaching
A. Morrison and D. McIntyre

Teachers and Teaching

A. Morrison and D. McIntyre

Penguin Books

Penguin Books Ltd, Harmondsworth,
Middlesex, England
Penguin Books Inc., 7110 Ambassador Road,
Baltimore, Md 21207, U.S.A.
Penguin Books Australia Ltd, Ringwood,
Victoria, Australia

First published 1969
Reprinted 1969
Copyright © A. Morrison and D. McIntyre, 1969

Made and printed in Great Britain by
C. Nicholls & Company Ltd
Set in Monotype Plantin

Penguin Science of Behaviour

This book is part of an ambitious project, the *Penguin Science of Behaviour*, which covers a very wide range of psychological inquiry. Many of the short 'unit' texts are on central teaching topics, while others deal with present theoretical and empirical work which the Editors consider to be important new contributions to psychology. We have kept in mind both the teaching divisions of psychology and also the needs of psychologists at work. For readers working with children, for example, some of the units in the field of Developmental Psychology deal with techniques in testing children, other units deal with work on cognitive growth. For academic psychologists, there are units in well-established areas such as Learning and Perception, but also units which do not fall neatly under any one heading, or which are thought of as 'applied', but which nevertheless are highly relevant to psychology as a whole.

The project is published in short units for two main reasons. Firstly, a large range of short texts at inexpensive prices gives the teacher a flexibility in planning his course and recommending texts for it. Secondly, the pace at which important new work is published requires the project to be adaptable. Our plan allows a unit to be revised or a fresh unit to be added with maximum speed and minimal cost to the reader.

Above all, for students, the different viewpoints of many authors, sometimes overlapping, sometimes in contradiction, and the range of topics Editors have selected will reveal the complexity and diversity which exist beyond the necessarily conventional headings of an introductory course.

B.M.F.

Contents

Editorial Foreword 9

Preface 11

1 The Study of Teachers' Behaviour 13

2 The Background and Training of Teachers 42

3 Teachers' Roles and Relationships 75

4 Motivation in the Classroom 121

5 Communication and Assessment 151

References 186

Index 199

Editorial Foreword

This is the first volume to be published in the *Penguin Science of Behaviour* series in the field of Social Psychology. In this part of the series a number of volumes are planned which will give a comprehensive coverage of Social Psychology, each written by active research workers, and providing an up-to-date and rigorous account of different parts of the subject. There has been an explosive growth of research in Social Psychology in recent years, and the subject has broken out of its early preoccupation with the laboratory to study social behaviour in a variety of social settings. These volumes will differ somewhat from most existing textbooks: in addition to citing laboratory experiments they will cite field studies, and deal with the details and complexities of the phenomena as they occur in the outside world. Links will be established with other disciplines such as sociology, anthropology, animal behaviour, linguistics, and other branches of psychology, where relevant. As well as being useful to students, these monographs should therefore be of interest to a wide public – those concerned with the various fields dealt with.

Teachers and Teaching makes an excellent beginning to the series. On the one hand it makes use of well-established laboratory-based findings, and of familiar concepts and methods in social psychology. In addition there are extensive references to field studies carried out in schools, many of them in Britain; the latter findings are less familiar to social psychologists, and are of fundamental interest and importance. The book should therefore be valuable both to students of social psychology and also to those concerned with education.

This volume deals with empirical problems such as the

most effective social skills for teachers to use, the training of teachers, social relationships in schools, the motivation of pupils and communication with and perception of pupils by teachers. Other aspects of the social psychology of education will be dealt with in a second volume by the same authors.

The authors are ideally equipped to write this book. They have been engaged in research for some years into questions of the attitudes of teachers, and the effects of teacher training, and are the authors of a number of research papers on these subjects. For a number of years they have also been occupied with the training of teachers, so are well acquainted with the practical aspects of the problems discussed here.

M.A.

Preface

At a time of lively examination of educational provision, when many changes are taking place in organization, curricula and teaching techniques, it is particularly important that we should have systematic information on the professional behaviour of teachers. The quality of education depends primarily upon their personal characteristics, their relationships with individual pupils and classes, and their skills in motivating pupils and managing classroom activities. Unless they are competent neither conventional instruction nor innovation is likely to be successful. Yet we are often in the position of knowing far less about the behaviour of teachers and the responses of pupils to variations in this behaviour than we do about the pupils they teach, the curricula, or the educational systems in which they work. In this situation, it is not only difficult to identify the kinds of skilled behaviour appropriate to particular classes and individuals, but we are also continually hampered in attempts to evaluate methods of professional training and to advise on ways in which these could be improved.

This book aims to draw together information from various sources on the behaviour of teachers in schools and classrooms. In doing this we have to recognize that the unevenness of evidence over different areas inevitably limits what can be said about some aspects of professional activities; however, it seems preferable to accept these limitations rather than to fill out what is obscure or uncertain with the kinds of subjective interpretation and prescription which sometimes pass for authority in works on teachers and teaching. The book begins by outlining some of the major ways of studying teachers, then goes on to consider some of the evidence we have on four topics: professional training, teachers' roles and professional relationships, classroom motivation, and communication and assessment.

In writing this book we are primarily seeking to give student teachers and practitioners a means of examining their professional behaviour against the background of their training, the schools they work in, and the classrooms in which they have professional and social relations with pupils. We hope it will also interest those who train our teachers and the parents of pupils in our schools.

We wish to thank Dr Michael Argyle for his encouragement and valuable comments; Mrs Dorothy F. Paddon for her editorial help; and our secretaries.

Acknowledgements

We should like to make acknowledgement to the following for permission to reproduce figures: for Figure 7 to Routledge and Kegan Paul; for Figure 2 to P. J. Runkel and the American Educational Research Association; for Figure 9 to *Scientific American*; and for Figure 4 to John Wiley and Sons.

1 The Study of Teachers' Behaviour

We are all teachers: a considerable part of our lives is spent in influencing the thoughts, feelings and behaviour of others – in raising our children, in our work, and in our social activities. Professional teaching, then, is not clearly distinguished from a number of other activities in many of its objectives and techniques, but does have particular priorities among its purposes and distinctive problems arising from the contexts in which it is done. However, for all our general or professional involvement as teachers, we still have difficulty in describing and analysing what it is we are doing and what influences we are having.

(a) One response to this situation is to argue that teaching is a unique personal activity, about which no useful generalizations can be made, mysterious in its successes and failures, and so subtle that current techniques of study are quite inadequate to explain it. An *(b)* alternative view which we shall examine is that, given adequate theoretical models and techniques of assessment, many aspects of teaching can be described in ways which lead to a better appreciation of current practice, and of how, in some respects, it might be improved.

Much of the traditional research on teachers and teaching arose from practical interest in finding better methods for selecting persons who would make 'good' teachers, and in improving the training and assessment of students and practitioners. Psychometric methods were widely used, and the assessment procedures, mass sampling of candidates and notions of long-term prediction already employed in educational and vocational selection were imported into the field. In recent years this type of study has been supplemented by attempts to provide detailed analysis of social and educational goals, so that clearer criteria can be applied to the study of teacher effectiveness, particularly where this is reflected in the responses of pupils. In addition, two further approaches have been increasingly used. On the one hand, patterns of inter-personal behaviour between teachers and their pupils have been studied by systematic observation in the classroom and in the laboratory. On the other, there has been increasing study of the effects on teachers' behaviour of the demands upon them of colleagues, parents and others. These three major approaches complement, and at some points overlap, each other. None the less, they involve basically different ways of thinking about the work of teachers, each with its own set of theoretical concepts, its implicit assumptions and its methodological techniques and problems.

Teacher Effectiveness

A dominant interest in research on teachers has been the question: in what respects do 'good' teachers differ in their personal characteristics from those who are not so good? It is a question which can be asked with varying degrees of sophistication.

The basic effectiveness model

Many studies have been concerned with the task of predicting the competence of teachers. Thus, if the personal characteristics of 'successful' and 'unsuccessful' teachers could be identified, then selection might be made at an early stage of the more promising candidates for training. The basic model for studies of this type had two components: *personal characteristics* and a *criterion of effectiveness* as a teacher.

Characteristics and Effectiveness Model

Personal characteristics	Criterion
e.g. general ability personality traits attitudes and interests social class origins	e.g. training performance supervisory assessments in teaching satisfaction with work pupil performance

The research tasks consisted of selecting potentially relevant personal characteristics, deciding upon a criterion of effectiveness, finding and applying appropriate assessment techniques to samples of student or practising teachers, and then computing correlations between the predictor and the criterion. Early studies were restricted in the number of variables examined, but later developments in computer processing have made possible the analysis of very large amounts of data obtained from assessment on perhaps a hundred variables (Warburton *et al.*, 1963).

The outcome of this approach is discussed later in dealing with professional training so that we are only concerned here with the model. Despite its popularity for research the results have usually been more promising than conclusive. In effect, the approach has been too restricted in its range of predictors and too gross in its applied techniques; the different contexts in which teachers work are not considered, so that many of the factors which are involved in shaping teachers' responses to teaching and their pupils' immediate and later behaviour are inevitably left out; an indirect assessment of personality characteristics takes the place of any direct study of the subtleties of classroom behaviour; and the lack of carefully defined criteria, appropriate to teaching situations, and of objective assessments against these, add uncertainty to research findings.

An extended framework

Many influences bear upon the educational careers of
pupils and a number of general models have been proposed
which take account of teacher, pupil and environmental
variables. Mitzel (1957) has suggested that the following
elaboration of the simple effectiveness model represents a
minimal area of interest for any research concerned with
the prediction of teacher effectiveness:

Type 1 Variables – Prediction sources
Personality characteristics of teachers
Training
Type 2 Variables – Contingency factors
Pupil: individual differences
Type 3 Variables – Classroom behaviour
Teacher behaviour } considered in relation to behaviour
Pupil behaviour } outside the classroom
Type 4 Variable – Criteria
Pupil growth: various dimensions, e.g. reading, social maturity,
classroom attitudes

Hence Mitzel stresses the major significance of pupils'
characteristics (Type 2 Vars.) and the interpersonal situation of the classroom (Type 3 Vars.) in shaping the effect
of the teacher's personality and training experience (Type
1 Vars.).

Such designs are certainly more realistic about the
influences upon teachers and pupils, but their scope
restricts, in practice, the number of variables under each
head that can be included in a study, and even then large-
scale data collection and analysis procedures have to be
undertaken. In Britain, Wiseman (1964) has made very
effective use of the approach in his absorbing study of
education and environment, teasing out the relationships
of home, community and school influences upon the basic
achievement of pupils in primary and secondary schools.

Criteria of teacher effectiveness

What constitutes success, effectiveness, competence or a
high level of skills in a teacher? Is it whether he or his

pupils are happy or miserable, whether or not he gets promotion or whether they pass or fail an examination? What are the criteria against which to study the teacher's personality or behaviour? In the first place, the salience of criteria is not an absolute matter, depending as it does upon the evaluations of interested parties and further, upon the type of pupil, teaching subject, or stage in educational career that one is considering. Moreover, while some criteria are readily open to objective assessment, others, such as social maturity, personal adjustment or critical ability are extremely difficult to measure.

In an attempt to provide a basis for discussion of criteria, the American Educational Research Association (1952) produced the following scheme, in which criteria are arranged in a possible order of importance:

Teacher's effect on:

    pupil's achievement and success in life
    pupil's achievement in subsequent schooling
    pupil's achievement of current educational objectives

Parent's satisfaction with the teacher
Supervisor's satisfaction with the teacher
Teacher's opinions, values, attitudes
Teacher's knowledge of educational psychology
Teacher's emotional and social adjustment
Teacher's knowledge of methods of curriculum
    construction
Teacher's knowledge of subject matter
Teacher's interest in subject matter
Teacher's grades in practice teaching
Teacher's grades in education courses
Teacher's intelligence

Clearly this is a wide-ranging list, and the particular criterion we choose to employ will depend upon whether we are studying the teacher in training or in school, upon our evaluation of its relevance and importance, and upon the extent to which we can provide an appropriate form of assessment. In general, however, criteria of pupils' achievement, especially of current educational objectives, are of the greatest interest. But, achievement, even when stripped of such phrases as 'success in life' is difficult to specify and to assess. Thus, while we may not have too much difficulty in reaching the decision that the factual knowledge of pupils at the end of a course of instruction is one suitable criterion, and we find that we can construct an acceptable means of assessment, there is likely to be considerable disagreement over other objectives, such as 'social adjustment' or attitude change, both in defining what we mean and in creating assessment instruments.

A taxonomy of educational objectives

In an attempt to clarify the issues involved in defining possible educational goals, and in designing courses and assessment techniques which match these goals, Bloom and others (1956, 1964) have produced a taxonomy of educational objectives, divided into three major areas: (a) cognitive – objectives involving such processes as recall of simple information, comprehension of material, and original ways of thinking; (b) affective – objectives concerned with interests, appreciation, values and emotional tendencies; and (c) psychomotor – those involving motor skills, such as handwriting, use of tools and speech. The subject areas of the curriculum involve all three domains, but clearly mathematics and the sciences, for example, lay great stress on cognitive objectives; art, music and social studies have very important affective components; and the technical and commercial subjects emphasize certain motor skills. Having established this general framework for studying objectives, Bloom and his colleagues have tried to produce an ordering of more specific objectives within the cognitive and affective fields. Thus, in the cognitive one there is further classification into:

Knowledge: recall of specific facts, of methods and of processes, or of a pattern, structure or setting.

apply to teaching plan

Intellectual abilities and skills: organized modes of operation and generalized techniques for dealing with materials and problems. This section is broken down more specifically into:

Comprehension: translation, interpretation and extrapolation.

Analysis: analysis of elements, analysis of relationships, analysis of organizational principles.

Synthesis: arranging and combining parts to constitute patterns and structures; production of a communication, plan of work, set of abstract relationships or hypotheses.

Evaluation: judgements about the value of material and methods for a given purpose; evaluation on the basis of logical accuracy and consistency; comparison of major theories and generalizations.

A great deal of the interest already shown in this taxonomy has come from workers involved in curriculum development and in assessment techniques; however, it also has a valuable place in research on the behaviour of teachers where it may introduce a much-needed precision in the definition of possible outcomes of this or that piece of behaviour. For example, what associations, if any, can be established between pupils' skills in comprehension or evaluation and the teacher's verbal behaviour, especially in its logical aspects? How do particular personality characteristics of the teacher bear upon such affective objectives as pupils' willingness to comply with sensible regulations, their acceptance of responsibility towards others, or upon changes in their social attitudes and behaviours?

When, hopefully, we have overcome the difficulties of defining our criteria there is still the problem of constructing appropriate assessment techniques. In general, our criteria are going to be concerned with the pupils' achievement of current educational objectives, although these cannot be isolated from more long-term achievements. Some of these current objectives may be fairly readily specified, for example, acquisition of a body of factual information in geography or history, and in such cases it is relatively easy to construct objectively marked tests. The same is true for some of the more complex areas such as reading skills and verbal reasoning. Thus, there are highly reliable instruments which will allow us to assess pupil 'gain' under different teacher conditions; and the tests provide us with a useful sampling of actual educational behaviours. Commonly, then, criteria of these sorts have been employed because such aspects of pupils' achievements interest us very much – we want to know whether this or that kind of teaching does or does not relate to how much the geographical information or the reading of pupils has improved. However, where the criteria concern some of the more advanced cognitive skills it is often very difficult both to define what we mean and, consequently, to produce appropriate test instruments. Suppose we were to argue for the superiority of one form of teachers' behaviour for developing divergent modes of thinking in pupils: what are we to understand as divergent thinking and how can we assess it? Conventional instruments are, almost by definition and form, convergent. We may, then, have to develop measures which elicit a variety of open-ended answers, difficult to score reliably, and involving highly evaluative judgements on our part as to whether they provide adequate sampling of something called divergent thinking.

The greatest difficulties of assessment undoubtedly lie in the areas of social attitudes, moral development, social maturity and personality traits. Instruments for assessing racial attitudes or moral judgements, for example, may or may not be very reliable, but even supposing that they are thoroughly designed they remain verbal samplings of sets of beliefs and evaluations which may have little relation to the actual behaviour of pupils. Particular difficulties exist then in areas of very great educational interest, where we should very much like to know what influences teachers have on the long term social behaviour of their pupils. Ideally we would want to carry out careful sampling of behaviour, but it is not easy to do this in the general circumstances of pupils' school and out-of-school lives, so that we have to depend upon the indirect methods of pencil and paper tests, or upon very general observational assessments in school, for example, of 'social climate' of groups, or upon controlled laboratory experiments.

Ratings of teachers

While the development and achievements of their pupils are recognized as being the ultimate criteria of teachers' effectiveness, it is often difficult to plan an investigation in which the pupils of all the teachers concerned are comparable in their backgrounds and initial abilities. Where this cannot be done, comparisons among teachers on the basis of achievement of pupils become complicated and of doubtful validity. Because of this, it has been common for researchers to use more immediate criteria of the competence of teachers, most often the degree to which supervisors or other observers are satisfied with teachers' work. Sometimes judgements of teachers' general competence have been used, but increasingly researchers have attempted to define several distinct aspects of teachers' performances and to seek assessments on each of these aspects.

One technique which attempts to systematize such judgements of teachers is that of the rating scale, which owes much of its popularity to the fact that it is familiar to teachers as well as to researchers, and is easy to construct and to apply. Such scales usually take the form of a heading, descriptive of the characteristic to be rated, followed beneath by a three, five or seven point linear scale on which the rater makes an entry appropriate to his judgement of the person being rated. Additionally, the categories on the scale may be given verbal labels, such as 'highly persistent', 'persistent' or 'lacking in persistence', or more precise behavioural descriptions. And, the rater may be given instructions to make his ratings of persons conform to an approximately normal distribution about a mean for the group to which they belong.

Despite their popularity several objections can be raised against rating scales. One of their more serious limitations when used for assessing the classroom behaviour of teachers is that an extensive amount of information about what has gone on has to be reduced to subjective and impressionistic endorsements on a few scales. Since they are heavily dependent upon the subjective impressions formed by the individual rater their reliability from one occasion of rating to another by the same rater, or between two or more raters on the same occasion, is highly variable. Also, when the rater is presented with several supposedly distinct characteristics to assess he may in fact be unable to distinguish between them, leading to a tendency to rate an individual as 'high', 'average' or 'low' on most of them. Finally, the information available to the rater can vary very much from one characteristic to another and from one individual to another.

The use of rating scales need not be ruled out – and for some purposes there may be no practical alternative – provided that care is taken in the choice of characteristics to be rated, in giving instructions to raters, and in training them to appreciate what they are doing. However, this technique is increasingly being replaced or supplemented by systematic observation and coding of classroom behaviours of teachers and pupils.

Teachers' reports of their own characteristics

A third set of criteria which have been widely used in assessing teachers is that of their opinions, values, attitudes and personality characteristics, where it is assumed that a particular trait, for example, child-centred or authoritarian teaching, is characteristic of a good or a bad teacher. Such traits are commonly measured by self-report paper-and-pencil tests which, when they are carefully constructed, have the advantages that they are easy to administer and to score objectively for large numbers of individuals, and have high reliability. A major limitation, however, is that they may have low validity as indicators of behaviour in particular circumstances, in the classroom or elsewhere; and it is often difficult to establish how valid they actually are. Also, in the case of attitude measures, the item content may quickly become dated or be inappropriate for some group of subjects. Furthermore, when people believe that they are being judged 'better' or 'worse' on the basis of their responses, it can be very easy for them to present a desirable picture of themselves. Such tests are primarily useful for making broad groupings of subjects for experimental purposes, and for testing candidates in training; closer examination of their actual teaching behaviour may then reveal related differences, as have been found, for example, with such personality characteristics as cognitive flexibility – rigidity (Harvey *et al.*, 1966).

As might be expected, the attitudes to educational issues of teachers in training and service have attracted interest as criteria upon which teachers might be assessed. The best known assessment instrument of this sort is the Minnesota Teacher Attitude Inventory, which has commonly been used as a global measure of permissive and child-centred teacher attitudes (Cook, Leeds, and Callis, 1951). Factor analysis of its items shows that it covers five sub-areas: 'modern' versus 'traditional' attitudes to class control; favourable versus unfavourable attitudes to pupils; permissiveness versus punitiveness towards particular forms of pupil behaviour; rejection of pupils; and desire to control versus inclination to let pupils do as they wish. In Britain, Oliver and Butcher (1962) have developed a set of three scales of educational opinions: naturalism–idealism, bearing particularly upon child-centred versus teacher-centred attitudes to pupils; radicalism versus conservatism, which deals with more general educational policies affecting schools; and theoretical–practical, comparing opinions on educational objectives. Both measures have useful applications in examining comparative opinion change and changes in opinion over time with student teachers and other sectors of the community, but they are limited indicators of the classroom behaviour of teachers.

Teacher–Pupil Interaction

Research on teaching has neglected the fascinating diversity of personal goals, of social and professional techniques, and of relationships in the classroom, yet it is in the detailed analysis of the behaviour of teachers and pupils towards each other that we are most likely to find answers to some of the most pressing questions. For example, how can we explain the relative competence of some teachers as compared to others, how can we specify clearly ways of resolving difficulties in the motivation and behaviour of pupils, and how can we acquire the detailed information we need for the improvement of professional training?

The study of classroom interaction requires both different concepts and different methods, depending as it does more on the work of social psychologists than on that of educationalists. To take one example of relevant work in social psychology, Argyle (1967) has put forward a model which draws upon important parallels between the performance of serial motor skills (for example, skills needed for playing tennis or for riding a bicycle) and the performance of social and professional 'skills'. Such common features are (a) the possession of fairly specific *goals* to be achieved, (b) the selective perception of *cues* as to the outcome of current acts, (c) the *processing* of information on the outcome, and, (d) the *translation* of information into plans for further acts, drawing here upon learned repertoires of social and professional techniques.

A basic feature of this and other similar models is the *feedback of information* from the effects of the 'performer's' own behaviour upon that of the other person; this feedback has the function of regulating and guiding his subsequent acts.

Runkel (1958), concerned specifically with the teacher and pupil in the classroom, has suggested a simple framework, consisting essentially of two identical components, one for teacher and one for pupil, connected in an information feedback cycle.

The steps in the model can be described by taking the teacher's component alone (Figure 1).

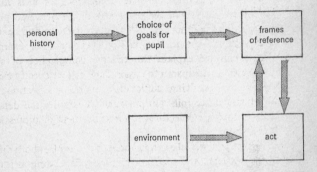

Figure 1. Some determinants of classroom acts (adapted from Runkel, 1958)

The teacher has personal needs and goals, represented here by his *personal history*, which in turn influence his *choice of goals* concerning the pupil. His *frames of reference* represent standards, derived from personal upbringing and professional experience, against which he makes assessments of his *acts*, of the acts of his pupils, and of the relevant features of the *environment*. These assessments in turn lead to the choice of further acts.

The complete model with its two components and the connexions between them is shown in Figure 2. The feedback of information is an essential feature at two stages: within the teacher's component, where there is self-assessment of behaviour; and between teacher and pupil, where the teacher receives information on the pupil's acts. Thus, there is a cyclical description of the relations between the teacher and the pupil in which their acts are seen as inter-dependent. This inter-dependence will, of course, vary in extent, as will also the particular patterns of interaction, upon many factors; upon the goals and techniques which the teacher and the pupil bring to the situation, upon how far their goals and techniques are compatible or contradic-tory, and upon the information each receives and the uses to which it is put.

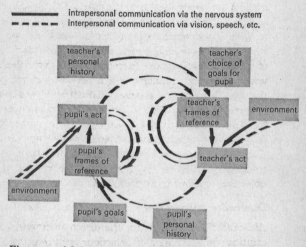

Figure 2. *A brief model for pupil-teacher interaction (Runkel, 1958)*

Models of this kind can be criticized on several grounds: they suggest that teaching is a more conscious decision-making process than is the case in actual encounters; they are difficult to use at more extensive levels than that of one person interacting with another; and even at a two-person level they indicate variables which would in practice be extremely difficult to encompass and to measure.

However, these difficulties do not detract from the

heuristic value of the model. We are encouraged to look at such matters as person perception, information feedback, stereotyping, sensitivity to pupil needs, social skills in specific contexts and teachers' expectations of pupils; all these are at the heart of day-to-day classroom events, but are largely neglected in much research. These models force us to look at what teachers and pupils do rather than to construct tenuous general hypotheses which are based on assumptions as to what happens in the classroom. Finally, they encourage us to consider teachers' behaviour as a set of rather specialized instances of general social techniques and skills, and so help to establish ways in which teaching is similar to or different from other forms of social and professional interaction. This might seem an unnecessary point to make were it not commonly argued that teaching is not a number of distinctive techniques, with specifiable patterns and levels of behaviour necessary for skilled performance, but something that most people, on the basis of their general repertoire, can do competently. This is an unresolved issue which lies at the roots of teaching as a profession, as well as being central to the objectives and methods of professional training.

Observation and description of classroom behaviour

Although the arguments for the direct observation, description and assessment of behaviour are strong, the bulk of research, in attempting to jump from personal characteristics of teachers to pupils' achievements, has largely ignored the detailed study of events in the classroom. For research concerned with pupil–teacher interaction, however, such detailed observation is essential. Practical difficulties inhibiting this type of approach in the past have been the costs involved in extensive observation and in analysis of the data obtained, and the reluctance of some teachers to allow observers into their classrooms. But while these practical difficulties are decreasing, there remain problems about the choice of areas of behaviour for observation. Classroom behaviour is so complicated, occurs on so many levels, so rapidly, and with so many individuals that a representation of even a small part of the events is difficult.

One technique is to use a carefully constructed rating schedule. The observer sits in the classroom, giving close attention to the areas of behaviour covered by the schedule, then, at the end of the session, goes away and attempts to distil his impressions into a number of ratings. Some objections to ratings have already been made, but where trained observers are used the technique can provide reliable information in large-scale studies where broad comparisons are being made between styles of teacher behaviour. The outstanding example of this post-session rating technique and its application is in Ryans' Teacher Characteristics Schedule and in his work on major classroom behaviour patterns of teachers (Ryans, 1960). However, a mass of impressions has somehow to be reduced to a few assessments; the process of observation is not separated from subjective assessment by the same individual; and, since there is no direct record of incidents or their sequences, actual interaction between teacher and pupil cannot be analysed.

In view of the limitations of post-session impression rating, several investigators have turned their attention to the development of methods of immediate recording of major types of overt behaviour in the classroom. In the simplest form this recording may consist of selecting some particular piece of behaviour for observation, then noting each occasion on which it occurs – the teacher smiles, a question is asked, or a pupil turns to talk to his neighbour – but more sophisticated procedures require the observer to pay attention to several classes of behaviour which fall within some major area of classroom activity such as the verbal behaviour of the teacher or the communication acts of pupils, and to enter all occurrences into an extensive record. In taking the case of the more elaborate procedures, it is clear that they present numerous problems in their development and practical operation, particularly in

deciding what is to be observed, how much can reasonably be attended to by an observer over a period of time,
and what sort of training and knowledge is required by
observers.

Two general forms of observation and recording have
been used. One, called *sign observation*, provides the
observer with a list of specific events, so that as and when a
particular event is observed he enters a tally in the appropriate section of the list. This form is illustrated by the
Observation Schedule and Record (OScAR) developed by
Medley and Mitzel (1958),[1] where the observer is provided
with a card for checking off particular activities as they
occur within five-minute observation sessions: for example,
'teacher works with individual pupil', 'teacher questions –
pupil answers', 'teacher leaves/enters room', or 'pupil
ignores teacher's question'. This procedure improves the
reliability of observations by reducing the difficulty of the
judgements required, does not demand very highly trained
observers, and separates the more or less objective process
of recording from that of scoring. The second form, called
category observation, provides the observer with a smaller
number of more general categories of behaviour and he is
required to observe what happens within a brief period
of time, to enter a tally in the category that best represents
the observed events, then to repeat the procedure for a
succession of such periods. A well-known example of this
technique is the scheme for interaction analysis developed
by Flanders (1964) in which the observer is given ten
categories of teacher and pupil verbal behaviour, and for
each three-second period of a total observation 'episode'
decides which category best represents the behaviour
observed in that period. Every 'episode', then, is initially
represented by a sequence of category numbers, which can
be transferred later to a matrix. The basic categories are
shown in Table I.

1. The *Report of The Primary School Survey* (Scottish Education Department, 1968) contains a very interesting section, written by J. Duthie, on the
use of a recent version of OS₀AR.

Table 1 Categories for Interaction Analysis (Flanders, 1960a)

Teacher talk	Indirect influence	1.	*Accepts feelings*: accepts and clarifies the feeling tone of the students in a non-threatening manner. Feelings may be positive or negative. Predicting or recalling feelings are included
		2.	*Praises or encourages*: praises or encourages student action or behaviour. Jokes that release tension, not at the expense of another individual. Nodding head or saying, 'um hm?' or 'go on' are included
		3.	*Accepts or uses idea of student*: clarifying, building or developing ideas suggested by student. As teacher brings more of his own ideas into play, shift to category 5
		4.	*Asks questions*: asking a question about content or procedure with the intent that a student answer
	Direct influence	5.	*Lecturing*: giving facts or opinions about content or procedure; expressing his own ideas, asking rhetorical questions
		6.	*Giving directions*: directions, commands or orders with which a student is expected to comply
		7.	*Criticizing, or justifying authority*: statements intended to change student behaviour from non-acceptable to acceptable pattern; bawling someone out; stating why the teacher is doing what he is doing; extreme self-reference

Student talk	8.	*Student talk – response*: talk by students in response to teacher. Teacher initiates the contact or solicits student statement
	9.	*Student talk – initiation*: talk by students which they initiate
	10.	*Silence or confusion*: pauses, periods of silence, periods of confusion

The matrix produced by entering tallies obtained from a single 'episode' or combination of 'episodes' makes it possible to derive several particular or more general 'scores' for such aspects of the verbal behaviour in a classroom as the total amounts of teacher or student talk, the extent to which the teacher employs direct influence, or the amount of sustained communication between students themselves. The 'scores' can most obviously be used to construct classroom profiles, but it is also possible to combine 'scores' from several categories, such as Flanders does when he combines categories 1 to 3, and categories 5 to 7 to calculate a ratio of indirect/direct teacher influence.

Flanders' scheme has proved effective from a number of points of view: it preserves a considerable amount of the actual behaviour, and, to a limited extent, the sequence of events; observer agreement on categorizing behaviours is high and observers can readily be trained in the reliable use of the categories; extensive data are obtained and are straightforward to analyse; and finally, the categories focus on aspects of the classroom which have been shown to be relevant to important variations in the performance of pupils. As such, his scheme demonstrates that systematic observation and recording can be a viable practical procedure and not just a luxury reserved for a team of highly skilled research workers.

The procedures so far outlined all require the human observer, and so it is necessary to compromise between what we might like to record and what we can reasonably expect a competent observer to do. No observer can provide us with lengthy sequences of detailed events over a number of major areas of activity, so that we cannot reasonably expect further advances in the scope of observer schedules and must look to other techniques. Given techniques that could provide much fuller behavioural records independently of a human recorder, the resulting mass of data could subsequently be scanned along any number of relevant dimensions; complicated sequences could be thoroughly examined, and coding reliability increased. The obvious answer would appear to lie in the various types of audio-visual system, and these methods in several forms have already been used by some investigators (Bellak, 1966; Kounin *et al.*, 1966). However, there are difficulties, some stemming from background noise in the classroom, others from the identification of speakers, from the siting and control of equipment, and, not least, from trying to order and interpret the mass of material obtained. Taking into account both the difficulties in effective use of sophisticated equipment and the great potentialities for accuracy and detail, the most promising applications of behavioural recordings are in carefully devised and controlled experiments done in the context of a fully equipped and permanent laboratory classroom.

Whichever classroom observation and recording technique is used the research worker ultimately has to decide which aspects of behaviour are to be studied and how content is to be classified. Where the teacher's behaviour is concerned the choice may lie among verbal behaviour, affective manner, characteristic roles, non-verbal social techniques and logical procedures in presentation and questioning. Study of the behaviour of pupils can concentrate upon verbal responses, attentiveness and task involvement, self-control or troublesome behaviour, and social relations with teacher or peers.

Much of the observational study done so far has focused upon social and organizational aspects of classes. These aspects are clearly important, but more attention needs to be given to the linguistic and logical characteristics of teachers' behaviour, to non-verbal techniques, and to classroom management techniques employed by teachers. Furthermore, if observational methods are to be used, and if they are to be employed both for describing what is done and for establishing associations between teachers' acts and pupils' responses, then the work undertaken must be closely geared to specific teaching contexts and to carefully defined categories of pupils.

Teachers' logical behaviour – the structure of the explanatory, evaluative and interrogative procedures they use to foster pupils' understanding of concepts and principles, and their skills in analysing problems and employing systematic approaches to the content of lessons – is of fundamental importance across all the subjects of the curriculum, but is currently of particular interest for the teaching of mathematics and science where modern syllabuses place much greater stress on grasp of principles and ability to apply them and less on the accumulation of specific knowledge. The teacher's logical behaviour in mathematics teaching has been the theme of work by Wright (1959), who has tried to produce an appropriate systematic observation procedure which could be used to analyse the teachers' methods and provide data for discriminating among the more or less skilled. However, from the attempts already made to analyse language in the classroom – whether from its logical, semantic or grammatical aspects – it is clear that there are as yet unresolved coding problems and that the necessary procedures require observers who are highly trained in observational techniques, language and subjects.

Observation techniques, however, seem unlikely to help in increasing our understanding of the less overt aspects of interaction in the classroom: processes of impression formation, the setting of teachers' expectations, and the processes of interpreting information from pupils. In these areas we have to rely less on controlled study of what is happening in on-going situations and more upon experimental manipulations of variables in classrooms or the laboratory.

The Teacher's Role

The approaches so far considered have been concerned firstly with relating the effectiveness of teachers, assessed in various ways, to their personal characteristics and background and secondly with the interdependence of teacher and pupil behaviour within the classroom. A teacher's behaviour is also, however, dependent upon the social and organizational framework within which he works. Formal and informal relationships with headmaster, colleagues, pupils' parents and others concerned with the work of a school are not only in themselves important features of a teacher's life, but may also have a considerable influence on his classroom behaviour. Most of these individuals are likely to have opinions as to how the teacher should do his job, and many of them are in positions to influence him.

In attempting to explain and to investigate this aspect of the teacher's job, the set of linked concepts known as 'role theory' has commonly been used. While there is fairly general agreement about the central concepts of role theory, there is little uniformity in the terminology used to represent these concepts, and the terms we employ may be used with rather different meanings by some sociologists and social psychologists.

Within any society an individual may be conceived as having several *positions*, e.g. daughter, teacher, youth club leader, etc., associated with each of which are certain corresponding *roles*, or appropriate patterns of behaviour. A role may be formally specified in some detail, as is generally the case for workers on an assembly line; but in so far as such formal specification is lacking, a role is determined by the *role norms*, or prescriptions of appropriate behaviour, and the *role expectations*, or conceptions of how people in such positions do behave, of all the 'relevant others' in related positions. The person filling a role is termed the *role incumbent* and these others form his *role set*, defined as the incumbents of all those roles which are interdependent with that of the focal person. A role does not usually involve precisely specified behaviours, but rather a limited range of behaviours which are acceptable in any particular context. Furthermore, the range of behaviours acceptable to different members of the role set may be different, and norms may differ considerably from expectations. There is a general, though not universal, tendency for the *role behaviour* of incumbents to conform to the norms and expectations of at least some members of the role set. Among the basic concerns of role theory are the explanation of the means whereby the behaviour of role incumbents is so influenced, and the discovery of which factors determine who exerts such influence and who does not.

A role is not dependent upon the personality of its incumbent. Just as the personality of an individual is conceived as being constant over the various roles which he fills, so the role associated with a position is conceived as being the same for the various individuals who may fill it. Role behaviour is thus a product of the role and the personality of its incumbent. Personality and role are not always, however, entirely unrelated. On the one hand, individuals may be attracted towards a particular role because they perceive it to be one which will satisfy their own personality needs. On the other, the effect of filling a role over a period of time may be that the individual's personality is influenced by his behaviour in that role. For example, some experienced teachers are observed to behave in other social contexts in ways thought by others to be appropriate only to their classroom role.

A concept which has attracted particular attention in the discussion of teachers' behaviour is that of *role conflict*. There are at least three different types of role conflict. *Inter-role conflict* results from the fact that individuals occupy several roles; these roles may demand different values, attitudes or loyalties, and situations may arise where it is not clear which role should be adopted. For example, a teacher who is associated with some of his pupils as a youth club leader or as a neighbour, is likely to experience occasions on which he has difficulty in choosing the appropriate behaviour towards these pupils. Inter-role conflict can also occur between such roles as class teacher, student of education, school administrator and parent because of their conflicting demands on an individual's time.

Intra-role conflict occurs when the norms and expectations of different members of the role set, as perceived by the incumbent, do not appear to him to be compatible. A teacher, for example, may feel that behaviour which is acceptable to his headmaster will be unacceptable to his colleagues, or that what is acceptable to his colleagues will be unacceptable to his pupils. Such conflict is a complex phenomenon, involving among other factors the extent of consensus among the role set, the accuracy with which the incumbent perceives their norms and expectations, the importance which he attaches to the approval of each group, and the degree of skill he shows in meeting a multiplicity of demands.

Thirdly, there may be conflict between the demands of a role and the needs of the incumbent's personality. Thus, a teacher with a strong need for achievement may be extremely unhappy in a role in which he is expected to emphasize 'the enjoyment of learning' rather than to seek tangible results. And the personality of a teacher who needs warm friendly relationships with others is likely to be incompatible with a role in which he must behave in a predominantly authoritarian way.

A model (Kahn *et al.*, 1964) for the study of roles in organizations such as schools is shown in Figure 3.

The four boxes in this figure represent events in a repeated sequence whereby 'role senders' (that is, significant members of an incumbent's role set – see above) hold expectations and norms for a role (I), in accordance with which they exert pressures (II) on the role incumbent, who experiences these pressures, gains fuller information about his role, and perhaps experiences role conflict (III), and responds in an attempt to cope with these experiences (IV). His response is then perceived by the role senders, evaluated against their norms, and possibly modifies their expectations; and the cycle begins again.

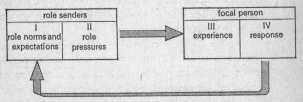

Figure 3. The basic cycle of interaction between role norms and role behaviour (adapted from Kahn, 1964)

This basic cycle of events occurs in a context of three other types of variable which affect it (see Figure 4):

Organizational factors – the division of labour, the hierarchical structure, the formal policies, etc. – are major determinants of the norms and expectations of role senders, and of the types of pressure which they can exert on the incumbent.

Personality factors of the incumbent influence the cycle in several ways. They influence the role senders' responses to him and the nature and strength of the pressures they exert upon him. His personality affects secondly the way in which he perceives these pressures, and thirdly, the nature of his responses to them. In addition, over an extended period, his personality may itself be changed by his experiences of pressures and by his responses to them.

Interpersonal relations between the incumbent and members of his role set – their power to influence him, bonds of respect or benevolence between them, mutual dependence, and styles of communication – have an influence upon the cycle parallel to that of personality factors. The perceptions and responses of both senders and incumbent depend upon, and in turn modify, the different

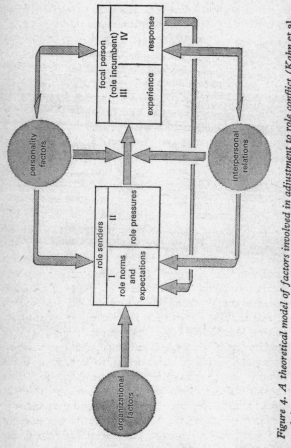

Figure 4. A theoretical model of factors involved in adjustment to role conflict (Kahn et al., 1964)

relations which the incumbent has with each of his role senders.

The conceptual framework provided by role theory and by the above model allows the formulation of a number of important questions about the behaviour of teachers. How do teachers' roles vary in accordance with aspects of school organization? What are the norms and expectations for teachers' behaviour held by various groups such as teachers, headmasters, pupils and parents, and to what extent is there agreement within and between such groups? How accurately do teachers perceive the norms held by various groups? How far does the role behaviour of teachers conform to these norms? What types of role pressures do different groups exert upon teachers? To what extent do teachers experience different types of role conflict, and what strategies do they use in attempting to resolve it? Which aspects, if any, of the teacher's role motivate people to become teachers?

Up to the present, research has predictably concentrated on those aspects which can be most easily studied: the norms and expectations held by various groups (e.g. Jenkins and Lippitt, 1951), and the accuracy with which teachers and other groups perceive the norms for teachers which others hold (e.g. Biddle *et al.*, 1966). Theoretical discussions of teachers' role behaviour, and in particular of role conflicts experienced by teachers, have not been lacking (e.g. Wilson, 1962), but empirical study of such conflict has tended to be anecdotal and unsystematic. Scientific methods of study developed in other contexts, however, could be applied to the teacher's role. The classic research by Gross and his colleagues (1958) into the role of school superintendents (local education administrators in the U.S.A.), for example, suggests one technique and indicates something of the potential of role theory research. A number of situations were selected with which all superintendents had to deal and for which conflicting norms within their role sets might be expected. Each superintendent was then asked to indicate the attitudes

which he perceived each of a number of groups to hold
with regard to these situations, whether he considered
each attitude to be 'legitimate', whether each group could
impose negative sanctions upon him if he did not conform
to their wishes, and finally how he himself normally acted
in such situations. When all the superintendents who saw
themselves as exposed to two incompatible norms were
considered, it was found that their strategies for resolving
the conflict, classified by comparing their behaviour with
their reports of legitimacy and sanctions, were highly
predictable on the basis of an independent assessment of
their personalities.

One problem which is particularly difficult to investigate
is the identification of ways in which the classroom
behaviour of teachers is influenced. It is of considerable
practical importance to discover both the processes whereby young teachers come to acquire relatively stable role
behaviour, and the factors which determine whether more
experienced teachers can be influenced to modify existing
patterns of behaviour. However, the many contexts in
which teachers are involved in social interaction with
various groups and individuals suggest that to investigate
such problems in the actual school context would involve
such elaborate research designs as to be impractical at
present; more progress can be expected through controlled
laboratory experiments which simulate aspects of the
teacher's situation. The problem of explaining the processes of influence involved would nonetheless be greatly
simplified if more were known about *who* has most influence
upon teachers' classroom behaviour. Once systematic and
objective procedures for observing and classifying classroom behaviour are more available, it should be relatively
easy to obtain such information.

Directions of Study

The three approaches to the study of teachers' behaviour
which have been described should not be considered as

conflicting or incompatible. Indeed, all three are necessary components in any long-term research strategy aimed at understanding, and thereby improving, teaching.

The value of most teacher effectiveness studies in the past has been limited by their attempts to predict teaching success directly from assessments of the personal characteristics of teachers without considering any intervening variables, by their unreliable assessment of rather gross features of classroom behaviour, and by their lack of attention to the varied contexts in which teachers work. A sounder basis on which to study the competence of teachers would be one which emphasized the detailed description of teachers' behaviour and analysed it in terms of the different social and cognitive skills which are required. Studies of classroom interaction are necessary so that these skills can be described, classified, and assessed validly and reliably, and the relevance of specific skills to different objectives discovered. Role-theory research is necessary to help clarify the objectives which a teacher's role requires him to seek in any one educational context, and also to find means for identifying role pressures which limit objectives or inhibit skilled teaching behaviour. Only then may it be possible to determine the extent to which teachers' personal characteristics, particular types of professional training and particular types of school and classroom organization, are predictive of competence in the various aspects of teaching. Thus the questions to which investigators were confidently seeking answers half a century ago can now be seen as answerable only on the basis of a great deal of research which has hardly begun.

2 The Background and Training of Teachers

The Characteristics of Teachers

The personal characteristics of teachers are major factors in shaping the social relationships, activities and achievements of our schools. Who are the teachers? How are they selected? How are they trained? This chapter examines aspects of the backgrounds and personalities of teachers, motives for choice of teaching as a career and the effects of professional training upon skills, abilities and attitudes.

Prior to those influences arising from the job of teaching itself, we can distinguish two general ways in which teacher characteristics are affected: firstly, the processes of selection, which involve both a person's decision to become a teacher and also the more formal procedures by which he is accepted for professional training and later considered to have successfully completed it; and secondly, the effects of the distinctive higher education and professional training undergone by student teachers.

Several factors are likely to operate in an individual's decision to teach. These are outlined in Figure 5.

These factors will vary in significance for different people, so that we should not expect to find any easy generalization about a 'teacher type' for whom we can specify a common pattern of background influences, motives, personality traits and skills.

The social and educational background of teachers

Educational background. In no Western society is the choice of a teaching career open to everyone. In Britain, entry to either of the two main avenues to a teaching qualification – courses in colleges of education and degree courses in universities – requires minimum academic

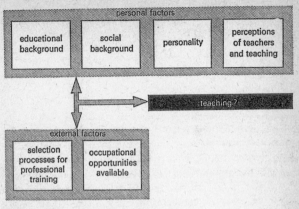

Figure 5. The decision to teach

standards which have meant that the great majority of entrants in recent years have had a selective secondary education, and have remained at school until at least the age of seventeen. Only about 10 per cent of each age group has had this sort of educational background.

In England and Wales especially, the minimum qualifications for entry to colleges of education are considerably less than those necessary for university entry. For those who wish some form of academic qualification but are not admitted to university, a college of education offers an accessible alternative. There is no reliable information as to the extent to which entrants to colleges of education are motivated in this negative way. However, there is a considerable overlap between the qualifications of entrants to the two types of institution, 40 per cent of college students having minimum university entrance qualifications; and only 22 per cent of college entrants in 1961 and 1962 had applied for university places.[1]

Of those graduates who have science degrees, those who become school teachers have, on average, rather poorer

1. Except where otherwise stated, figures quoted in this section are from the Report on *Higher Education* (Robbins), Appendix Two (B).

degrees than those entering other occupations, but this is only marginally true of arts graduates. If one includes the highly qualified group who continue post-graduate studies then, in many cases, go on to university teaching, the teaching profession as a whole gets a better than average selection of graduates.

Social background. The educational selection which occurs on entry to secondary school and less formally throughout secondary education is in large measure also a process of social selection, with a relatively small proportion of working class pupils successfully completing courses in selective schools. It is therefore inevitable that student teachers should tend to come from homes with above average socio-economic status.

Table 2 Social Class Distribution (Percentages) of Students by Fathers' Occupations, 1961–2 (*Higher Education*, 1963)

Social class category	Students' fathers				Economically active men Total population (*1961 Census*)
	Colleges of education		Universities		
	Men	Women	Men	Women	
1. Higher professional	5	8	17	20	4
2. Other professional, managerial	27	35	40	43	14
3. Clerical	16	14	12	11	12
4. Skilled manual	32	28	19	16	36
5. Semi-skilled manual	13	7	6	6	20
6. Unskilled manual	2	2	1	1	9
7. Not known	5	5	5	3	5

This bias toward middle class recruitment is much less for college of education students than it is for university students. Thus, 18 per cent of university students have fathers in higher professional occupations and 25 per cent have fathers in manual occupations, as opposed to 7 per cent and 40 per cent respectively for college of education students. While this may partly reflect the higher qualifications of university students, it is also possible that the three-year college course is seen by working class students as the quicker route to professional qualifications and earning power.

The middle class bias among college students is less marked for men than it is for women students. Data given by Ashley, Cohen and Slatter (1967a) suggest that this is also true of graduates entering teaching. On a five point scale of social class, 21 per cent of the male graduate students were from classes 4 and 5, compared with 8 per cent of female graduates and 9 per cent of females following a three year course. Considering graduate and non-graduate teachers, the heaviest recruitment is from social class 2, the category in which the majority of teachers are themselves placed. Ashley and his colleagues found that among the students with this background, 32 per cent had at least one parent who was a teacher, which is probably more than one would expect by chance. In addition many of the students from classes 3 and 4 had siblings who had entered the teaching profession. Thus it would seem that having a close relation who is a teacher may predispose one to teaching.

Sex. Teaching is a predominantly female profession, and this is increasingly the case the younger the pupil taught. Over 70 per cent of college students are women and the proportion of women graduates in arts or sciences who enter teaching is twice that of men graduates. This female bias has the effect of also increasing the bias in social class and towards arts subjects. It also has important implications for teacher-pupil relationships and other aspects of school education.

Personality characteristics. Despite a large number of

investigations, no consistent pattern of interests or of preferred pastimes has been found to distinguish student teachers from other students. Educational attitudes have not attracted the same attention, but what evidence is available (e.g. McIntyre and Morrison, 1967) again does not discriminate between student teachers and others. Evans (1952), however, studying the attitudes of sixteen-year-old pupils in secondary schools towards teaching as a career, found that, while other attitudes and interests did not discriminate, those who had the greatest liking for school as pupils most favoured the idea of teaching themselves. This indicates the considerable influence which teachers may have on the recruitment to their profession.

Those choosing teaching as a career have consistently been found to differ in their values from the population as a whole in two respects in particular: as a group they put less than usual value on what is seen as useful, efficient and economic, and more than usual value on personal relationships.

Many researchers have used personality inventories in the attempt to find distinctive characteristics of teachers. Contrary to some popular views, results have generally shown that teachers tend to be well-adjusted, emotionally stable, objective and sociable people. Such results are not, however, very revealing, since they could scarcely be said to discriminate teachers from other people. One particularly interesting result has been with one of the scales of the Minnesota Multiphasic Personality Inventory, known as the K scale, which assesses the general tendency of a respondent to assent to statements in the inventory. Teachers have been found in several investigations to score highly on this scale. Gowan (1955), reviewing results with the K scale, has suggested that it indicates 'some degree of social anxiety overlaid with reaction formation in which emphasis is directed towards control of self and adaptation to the needs and demands of others'. Thus teachers in general may be more inclined than most to behave in conformity with the social pressures which they experience.

Because of the educational selection involved in becoming a teacher, it is inevitable that teachers as a group should be well above average in intelligence; and numerous investigations have shown this to be the case. On the other hand, an equally consistent tendency in the results of American research is for the mean I.Q.s of students preparing to be teachers to be rather low compared with those of students preparing for other professions such as technology, medicine and accountancy. Similarly, the mean I.Q.s of students in British colleges of education tend to be lower than those of university students. Such general tendencies, however, hide a wide range of I.Q.s among teachers.

In almost every investigation of the personal characteristics of those who become teachers, greater differences have been found between different groups of teachers than between teachers as a whole and the rest of the population. Students intending to be primary school teachers, for example, tend to be more interested in people, to have more progressive educational attitudes and to be more sympathetic towards children than those who specialize in secondary school teaching; the latter tend to place more value on clear thinking and on finding out the truth, to be more interested in intellectual pursuits and to be more intelligent (according to measured I.Q.). Among secondary school specialists, values, interests and abilities tend to reflect the subject taught, student teachers of science and English, for example, having attributes more in common with research scientists and novelists respectively than with one another.

Experiences of home and school

Few results have emerged from research into the personal experiences of teachers before they enter the profession. Furthermore the validity of any results which are obtained is always questionable since all such studies have been retrospective; difference between teachers and others may reflect differential tendencies in their recollections rather than actual differences in their past experiences. Wright and Tuska (1966), however, found some interesting results in their comparison of the recollections of student-teachers with those of other students of childhood relationships with parents and teachers. Male student-teachers more often remembered unsatisfactory relationships with their fathers than did other male students. Also, together with intending female high-school teachers, they tended to remember their teachers as influencing them, and they also admired them more than they did their mothers, while the opposite was the case for other groups of students. Wright and Tuska interpret these results by suggesting that the choice of a teaching career depends on the identification of students with their parents or teachers as models; girls who wish to be elementary school teachers, for example, are likely to identify with their mothers (and see the job as a mothering job), but those who wish to teach in secondary schools tend to find their mothers inadequate models and instead to identify with their teachers. These results again suggest that the nature of the relationships which teachers establish with their pupils may be an important factor in determining how many and which of these pupils will become teachers themselves.

Reasons given for becoming a teacher

The decision to become a teacher is for most people conscious and deliberate, and those who become teachers are in general relatively intelligent and articulate young adults. How important are the reasons which people give themselves to explain their decision to become teachers, when compared with other less conscious motivations? To what extent do these reasons result from, or take cognizance of, the various personality characteristics which the decider has or believes himself to have? As yet, little is known in answer to these questions. Researchers have either concentrated on investigating the assessed characteristics of teachers or on their conscious motivations, without relating the two types of variable.

The reasons which students give for choosing a teaching career tend to vary according to social and economic conditions. The range of opportunities for employment, the prestige of the teaching profession, conditions of employment for teachers, and the influence of parents over their children's occupations can all be important factors in some contexts but not in others. Tudhope (1944) for example, found that the two most common reasons given for entering the teaching profession were its economic security, and advice from parents; but later investigations have not found the same importance being given to these factors.

Altman (1967), considering the motives of a group of mature students who were giving up other jobs to become teachers, found that the majority of them, although from working-class backgrounds, were in middle-class or lower-middle-class occupations, were successful in, and reasonably satisfied with, these occupations, and were unlikely to benefit financially from becoming teachers. Asked to rate the importance of ten different aspects of occupations, they rated 'opportunity to be helpful to others' as of considerably greater importance in teaching than in their current occupations and 'opportunity to make a good deal of money' as much less important. The opportunities to use abilities and aptitudes, and to be creative and original were also seen as more important in teaching.

Ashley, Cohen and Slatter (1967b) attempted to make a systematic analysis of the reasons given for entering teaching by students in a Scottish college of education. They found it possible to classify the 1,454 statements into five categories which emphasized, in order of the frequency with which they were mentioned, (1) the conditions of work of teachers, (2) interest in the task of teachers, (3) the satisfaction of personal needs, (4) the value of education to society and (5) negative reasons, such as inability to think of anything better. The relative importance attached to these five types of reason varied with the sex and socio-economic status of the student, and with the age-group he or she intended to teach. For example, students of lower socio-economic status and those who intended to teach in primary schools placed more emphasis on the task of teaching than did other sub-groups.

Implications

From the evidence we have summarized it is clear that, at least in terms of personality characteristics, 'the typical teacher' is not very different from 'the typical person'. This however represents a simplification of the situation, since it is also clear that those motivated to become specific types of teacher, such as teachers of infants or teachers of physical education, do tend to have distinctive attributes. One of the few general tendencies we have noted is for recruits to teaching to be people who have themselves enjoyed being pupils and who admired their teachers more than others did. This, together with a possible tendency for the children of teachers to become teachers, and the suggestion that teachers are in general more ready than most people to adapt their behaviour to accord with the expectations of those with whom they come into contact, presents a picture of teaching as a somewhat ingrown profession, which may therefore be inclined to perpetuate its practices from generation to generation in a way relatively impervious to outside influence.

It is, however, in their social class origins, their sex, and their educational background that those entering the teaching profession are most atypical. The predominantly lower-middle-class background of teachers has a variety of repercussions in their classroom behaviour, which we will examine more closely in later chapters; among these are the distinctive forms of language which are most commonly used in teaching, the standards of morals and manners, the attitudes and ways of using their time to which they expect their pupils to conform, and the educational objectives which they see as appropriate for different groups of pupils.

The sex of teachers is a factor which appears to have an equally pervasive influence on classroom relationships; among other things, it has been shown to affect the teacher's perception of pupils, the aspirations and attitudes of pupils, and the teacher's degree of involvement in the job of teaching. Therefore, it should be borne in mind that the majority of teachers, especially in primary schools, are women.

Almost all those who, up to the present, have become teachers in Britain have had a selective secondary education. On the one hand this may lead them to have especially great problems of communication with pupils of average or lower abilities; but on the other, student-teachers may have fewer preconceived ideas about how to teach less able pupils, and may therefore be more easily influenced in their thinking about this aspect of the job.

The Selection of Teachers

The prediction of teaching ability

Because of the prevalent shortage of qualified teachers, few authorities can afford to be highly selective in admitting students to professional training courses, or in employing teachers after they have been trained. As a result, the problem of prediction is currently of limited practical importance. Nevertheless, no other aspect of research on teachers has been more investigated, and the concern to identify the 'naturally able' teacher as early as possible has taken precedence over investigating methods of training.

Most of the predictive studies fall into two categories: those which use the personal characteristics and school attainments of would-be teachers as independent variables and college examination results and, in particular, teaching marks as the criteria; and those which use these college results in an attempt to predict teaching success on the job as rated by school principals, inspectors or others. The validity of any predictive study depends upon having as criterion an objective, reliable, and valid measure of the performance at issue. While other aspects of prediction are not central to this book, the judgements, attitudes and skills involved in the choice and use of criteria are directly relevant.

Teaching marks. In most studies the major criterion has been the college teaching mark, usually given on a five point scale, or a similar single assessment given by an observer of the practising teacher at work with his class. Some of the inadequacies of rating techniques have been outlined in the previous chapter. With teaching marks one added disadvantage is that we do not in general know what it is that tutors are assessing, or even what they think they are assessing. Robertson (1957) elicited the views of a variety of student supervisors and chose a sample of fifty attributes which were mentioned as being important for a teacher. He then asked eighteen supervisors in one training institution to rank these attributes in order of their importance in contributing to a high teaching mark. Correlations between the eighteen sets of rankings ranged from $0 \cdot 73$ to $-0 \cdot 16$, with a coefficient of concordance of $0 \cdot 38$. It is clear that even within the same institution, teaching marks given by different supervisors are not intended to mean anything like the same thing.

It is not surprising that supervisors should differ so much in their criteria of a 'good teacher'. Having no evidence on what sort of people are good teachers, and little on what sort of teaching is good teaching, each must rely on his own opinions. These opinions must reflect largely what each supervisor believes has been effective in his own teaching; and since each has a different personality, has different teaching experiences and, for lack of authoritative guidance, has formulated his conclusions from these experiences in his own way, it would be surprising if opinions did not differ radically.

When a supervisor has decided what he is assessing, how skilled is he at observing the things for which he is looking? Lantz (1967) compared the assessments made of students on reliable and well-tried classroom observation schedules by trained psychological observers with the ratings made on eight scales by the class teachers and by university supervisors. The scales and the observation schedules were both restricted to aspects of behaviour reflecting emotional climate in the classroom, and the directness and indirectness of the teacher's influence. Ratings made by the class teachers did not predict the scores derived from the observation schedules significantly better than chance; those of the supervisors, however, did allow for significant prediction, but the three multiple correlations were only 0·48, 0·59, and 0·46. To be an experienced teacher does not seem to imply any skill as an observer of teaching. Such skill does not come automatically or easily, and people must vary considerably in their ability to acquire it when left to their own resources. One of the unfortunate features of the current training situation is that it is almost unknown for tutors to be given any systematic training in these observational skills.

Where personal opinion plays such a large part, the degree of compatibility between the personalities of rater and ratee is likely to have a significant effect upon the judgement made. Start (1968) found that ratings of teaching ability made by the headmaster of teachers in a secondary modern school were related to the similarity of the personalities of headmaster and teachers as assessed by personality tests. Those who were most similar to and most different from the headmaster tended to be rated higher than others. The nature of the similarity or dissimilarity was also important. 'The headmaster saw the successful teacher ... as a more intellectual, less confident or less experienced version of himself, and one who has to draw from the head teacher's experience in the field.' It is probable that college tutors are similarly influenced by their personal relationships with students.

Finally, one may question the comparability of the student teaching situation with that of the employed qualified teacher. The low prestige of the student, his lack of intimate knowledge of the pupils and his lack of control over the normal classroom experiences of pupils must all affect the pattern of his teaching to an unknown degree. In addition, it is likely that college supervisors tend as a group to stress different qualities from those which are seen to be important by the schools. Bach (1952) found no relation whatsoever between ratings of various aspects of teaching given by supervisors and those given by school principals four months after the students had started teaching. Furthermore, the patterns of correlations between ratings on the various scales were quite different for the two groups. This suggests that, although the supervisors and the principals were using the same descriptive scales, they were interpreting these descriptions in two distinct ways, and focusing their attention on different aspects of the teaching they observed.

It must be concluded that teaching marks as currently given are of very little value as predictors of teaching ability, and are certainly inappropriate as criteria for attempts to predict the teaching ability of students. However, they continue to be used for both these purposes and also more generally in influencing the initial employment and future promotion of teachers.

Predictive studies. The general use of rating scales, and in particular of all-inclusive teaching marks, as criteria suggests that it is unlikely that consistent results have been found in investigations attempting to predict teaching ability. Probably the most comprehensive study of the prediction of student success in training is that of Warburton, Butcher and Forrest (1963). Students in a university department of education were assessed at the start of their one year course on eighty-three variables, including interests, attitudes, values, personality traits, academic achievements and aspects of their personal histories and home backgrounds. The two main criteria were their final marks in teaching and educational theory. Only seven variables were significantly correlated with final teaching marks, three of these being general assessments of their abilities based on interviews and knowledge of their academic attainments, the others being degree class and the personality traits of conscientiousness, self-control and sensitivity. Of these significant correlations the highest was 0.28. Correlations with the theory mark were generally higher, the highest being 0.57 with degree class.

One other British study is of particular interest. Cornwell (1958) theorized that a major aspect of teaching ability was skill in interpersonal relations, that the degree of such skill would be shown in the relations of student teachers with one another, and that the effects of such skill would be found in the frequency with which students were selected by their peers as associates and as hypothetical colleagues. He administered a series of carefully prepared sociometric tests to seventy-three students in their second term of a six term training course, and found that the measures so obtained correlated 0.57 with the final teaching mark given eighteen months later. This approach has not so far been replicated, and the results may only mean that supervisors were attracted by the same qualities in students as were other students; but it is interesting for its stress on the social interaction view of teaching, for the unusually high correlation found, and in that it is one of the few studies in this area which starts from even a minimal theoretical basis, rather than being a blind statistical exercise.

The second kind of predictive study is that which uses teaching marks and other college assessments as predictors of 'on the job' success, the criteria being ratings of teachers made by school principals and others. Tudhope (1942) found a correlation of 0.81 between the college assessments of ninety-six students and those made by school inspectors after a median teaching experience of nine years. This result is something of an anomaly, however, and the majority of studies have produced results of the same order as those of Wiseman and Start (1965), these being correlations of 0·28, 0·28 and 0·07 respectively for grammar, secondary modern and primary school teachers. At least one British study was never submitted for publication, apparently because it was thought unwise to publicize the low correspondence between college assessments and those by school inspectors!

The Professional Education of Teachers

In the United Kingdom, the great majority of teachers receive their initial professional education either in three year courses in colleges of education or in one year courses for university graduates and others with specialist qualifications. In England and Wales, the one year courses are in university departments of education, while in Scotland they are in the colleges of education.

At the start of this century, the instruction given in teacher training colleges was in keeping with the teaching procedures of the elementary schools for which their students were being prepared. Since the teaching in these schools was highly formalized and its objectives were mainly the accumulation of information and the inculcation of habits, the college instruction was largely aimed at the learning of large numbers of detailed rules of pedagogy for all specific contexts. In the last half-century, however, there has been a complete change of emphasis. According to modern educational precepts, the individual interests and 'needs' of pupils should determine much of the activity in the classroom, and the personal relationships between teacher and pupils are of fundamental importance. In such a context, precisely defined teaching techniques and procedural rules appear to be quite out of place. The view has therefore increasingly been taken that intellectual competence, human understanding and desirable educational attitudes are more important attributes to be fostered by college education than is the mastery of any teaching skills. Jeffreys (1961) expresses a widely held view when he says that 'we think it is more important, in training teachers, to produce well-educated people than to produce technically competent practitioners'.

To achieve these new objectives, a large proportion of the time in three-year college courses has been devoted to the study of 'academic' subjects, treated in much the same way as they would be in university undergraduate courses. Another aspect of these more 'liberal' courses has been a greater emphasis on the theoretical study of education, involving such disciplines as philosophy, history, comparative education and, most of all, psychology.

Psychology in teacher education

Since all teaching is concerned with changing the behaviour of pupils in one way or another, one may view the professional expertise of a teacher as consisting largely in his skill as a type of applied psychologist. Certainly the study of psychology has, ever since it became a subject of scientific study, figured increasingly in the training of teachers. But although there are wide variations among colleges in the content, methods and goals of their teaching of psychology, one may question how far these have generally been suited to the task of preparing skilled teachers.

One may first note that the aspects of psychology which have been stressed in college courses have tended to be the same as those predominating in general courses on the psychology of human behaviour in universities: perception, learning, thinking, cognitive development, individual differences (Peel, 1962). In contrast, social and clinical psychology have been relatively neglected; and yet it is in these areas, for example with problems of communication, motivation, individual–group relations and maladjustment, that most teachers face their most difficult practical tasks.

Secondly, the emphasis has been on the behaviour of children and of pupils, with little mention of teachers' behaviour. It is certainly desirable that teachers should understand the behaviour of their pupils; but unless they also appreciate how this behaviour is related to their own, and are able to plan their activities so as to elicit the pupil responses they want, such understanding will add little to their professional ability. Furthermore, a knowledge of general patterns of teacher behaviour and of concepts which may be used in their description and explanation are important tools for anyone attempting to examine and consequently improve his own teaching.

Finally, and perhaps most fundamentally, psychology has normally been considered only as part of the theoretical education of students, not part of their practical training. The aim has seemed to be that students should acquire a *knowledge* of psychology, most teaching consisting of the communication of psychological concepts and evidence by lectures. The training of students in such psychological skills as observation, diagnosis, communication and class management has not usually been attempted by lecturers with psychological training and experience. This academic approach to the teaching of psychology is no doubt a valuable part of the general education of students, but as a means towards increasing their effectiveness as teachers it seems to rely too much on their own abilities and initiative. In training courses for other occupations, such as advertising and industrial management, much more direct attempts are made to utilize psychological insights in increasing practical skills.

Methods lectures

While students no longer have to learn such detailed rules for teaching, some instruction in the colleges is intended to give them practical guidance about 'teaching methods'. No systematic information is available about how such courses are organized or what is taught in this context, but practices probably vary considerably among colleges. Among topics commonly discussed are techniques of discipline and class management, the use of audiovisual aids, planning of work, and specific methods such as

'Cuisenaire', 'the patch method', and the use of the initial teaching alphabet. Very little research has been done on some of these aspects of teaching; but since the majority of lecturers engaged in this work are recruited on the basis of their teaching experience and ability, they tend in any case to be ill-equipped to assess psychological theories and any research results which might be relevant. In their teaching, they are therefore forced to rely largely on their personal experience, accounts of the experiences of others, and on 'common sense'. There tends to be therefore a lack of theoretical organization in such courses, and, although giving rules for teaching is not consistent with the attitudes of most college lecturers, much of the instruction given is in the form of a series of practical hints and suggestions which, being pragmatically justified, are not conceptually related to one another.

Between these practical suggestions and the concepts and theories of psychology and of educational philosophy there is often a wide gap. The problem is that theoretical courses are not about teaching, and that methods courses, which *are* about teaching, have no theoretical foundation. In many colleges there are integrated education courses involving 'philosophy', psychology and methods; but the solution to this problem must involve linking concepts rather than merely linking timetables. Bruner (1966) comments that 'there is a lack of an integrating theory in pedagogy, ... in its place there is principally a body of maxims'. While this gap remains and college lecturers are unable to bridge it, it seems unlikely that students will be able to do so for themselves. In these circumstances, it should not surprise us if the theoretical study of education is dismissed as irrelevant to the practice of teaching, and if, for lack of sufficiently coherent conceptual organization, the many specific suggestions of methods lecturers are poorly assimilated to the teaching repertoires of students.

Teaching practice

Between one tenth and a quarter of the time of college

courses is devoted to teaching practice and observation in schools. Within the limitations of students' age-groups and subject specializations, they are usually allocated to schools at random; and in primary schools, they are normally attached to specific teachers, again virtually at random. As students progress through their training course, it is normal for them to be given a gradually increased amount of responsibility in their practice teaching, but this is left largely to the discretion of the schools. Teachers are expected to advise students about their teaching, but they are rarely given either guidance or training for this task. The skilfulness of the teaching which students observe, and the nature and amount of advice they receive, must inevitably vary widely; it is hoped that, by being with several different teachers during their professional education they will observe a variety of styles and some 'good' teaching. Students must also vary in their ability to observe what is happening in classrooms, and to learn from their observations. Without some training in this complex skill, which is very rarely given, students, accustomed as they are to a very different role in classrooms, are unlikely to take a sufficiently analytic view to notice and reflect upon any but the most dramatic of classroom incidents. It is not easy at any one time to perceive the on-going problems with which the teacher is faced, how he attempts to cope with these, and how different pupils react to his various actions, or any of the other aspects of the constant social interaction in a classroom. Even were such training given, it is questionable whether this exposure to the total complexity of the teaching process is an efficient way for students in the early part of their training to acquire an understanding of it.

For about half an hour a week, on average, students on teaching practice may be visited by supervisors from their college. One purpose of these visits is to assess the student's teaching ability, but the major objective is to allow supervisors to advise students about their teaching. The relative rarity of these occasions, together with the threat of assessment, can however lead to acute anxiety for the student and usually leads to special preparation in several ways. Thus the teaching observed is unlikely to reflect the usual teaching of the student. No evidence is available as to how much advice supervisors give students, or on what aspects of teaching they tend to concentrate. Nor is there evidence about changes induced in students' teaching by advice given. What is observed and commented upon and the value of the advice given depend virtually entirely upon the characteristics and intuitive skill of the individual supervisor. In recent years, increasing use has been made of standardized schedules for describing the different aspects of students' teaching. While this may not increase the value of the advice given, it is likely to encourage a more balanced attention to different aspects of students' teaching than can be achieved without such guidance.

Although research evidence is lacking, there seems good reason to believe that the procedures outlined above are crude and inefficient means by which to train students in the practical skills of teaching. To remedy this situation, a variety of innovations have been suggested with the objectives of making students' observation of teaching more fruitful, helping them to assess their own teaching in a more analytic way and thus to modify it, and giving them assistance in relating their theoretical studies to classroom phenomena.

One possibility is the selection of experienced practising teachers who could be trained in observing students in their classrooms, in advising them about their teaching, and in helping students to benefit from observing, criticizing and discussing with them their own teaching. Another is suggested by Sarason, Davidson and Blatt (1962) who, with a student seminar, watched a teacher at work with her class through a one-way screen at regular periods during the session. The students were thus able to discuss on the spot the problems and incidents they observed, and also to learn about the inadequacy of their own observations and so to improve them. A third is that suggested by Flanders (1963), that students should be taught ways of assessing pupils' perceptions, achievements, etc., and also the skills of observation for the type of interaction analysis he has perfected, and that they should be assigned to teaching practice in pairs. They would plan their teaching together and alternately one would teach and the other observe and collect the data they considered relevant. Thus they would learn about their own teaching in detail, they would learn to observe a class in a systematic and relatively objective way, and they would learn the value of self-assessment. The effectiveness of such approaches needs, of course, to be assessed; but it is difficult to believe that they would not all be valuable as ways of replacing or supplementing the mere exposure to classrooms at work which has been customary.

In particular, the complexity of the activity in a class-room at any one time, and the many aspects of teaching, are such that a student beginning to learn how to teach cannot give his attention to more than a small part of it; and, whether observing or teaching, he is likely to be overwhelmed by this complexity, to retain only very vague general impressions and consequently to learn little. It would be desirable, especially in the early stages of training, to reduce the situation to manageable proportions. One way of doing this is by simulating carefully planned classroom situations, with students playing various roles, and using this as a basis for analysis and discussion. A more ambitious approach, which is being increasingly used in the United States, is 'micro-teaching'. The student attends a lecture on a specific aspect of teaching, such as 'using the pupils' questions', and then takes a class of about six pupils for twenty minutes, giving particular attention to this aspect. He then sees a videotape of his teaching, discusses it with a supervisor, and an hour later tries again with another 'micro-class'. Such approaches as this high-light the need for teaching in various contexts to be analysed so that major constituent skills become apparent, and also the need for explicit, meaningful and reliable criteria by which relative mastery of these skills can be assessed. Unless one can know which aspects of one's teaching are weak, one cannot give them the necessary attention.

Staff and teaching methods

With only a few exceptions, lecturers in colleges of education are experienced schoolteachers. Probably as a result of this, they tend to be older than university teachers, the respective median ages in 1962–3 being forty-six and thirty-eight.[1]

The qualifications of college lecturers cover the same range as those of the teaching profession as a whole, although on average college lecturers are a good deal more highly qualified than schoolteachers. Similarly the preponderance of women in the teaching profession is reflected, slightly more than half of the teaching staff being women, as opposed to only 10 per cent of university teachers.

The student–staff ratios of colleges of education reflect their origins as normal schools with no academic pretensions, rather than their present functions and responsibilities. In 1962–3 the average for colleges in England and Wales was 11·2, and for the Scottish colleges which are much larger on the whole, 16·4. In comparison the ratio for the universities at the time was 7·5. Perhaps the most appropriate comparison is with the medical faculties of universities, which like the colleges of education are concerned both with the academic education of students and with their practical training for a profession concerned with diagnosing and meeting the needs of individual people; for these faculties, the national student–staff ratio was 6·0. According to University Grants Committee figures for 1966–7, the university departments of education are also comparatively badly off, having the highest student–staff ratio of all sections of the universities.

One of the effects of these student–staff ratios is that, while medical teachers are reported to spend an average

1. Unless otherwise stated, evidence quoted in this section is from the Report on *Higher Education*, Appendix III.

of fourteen hours a week on research, the amount of research done in colleges of education is negligible. Other effects are in the restricted range of teaching methods. Apart from teaching practice and practical classes in such subjects as art and physical education, nearly all the teaching received by college students is through lectures, with some little time being spent in discussion periods with ten or more students. Organized individual and small group tutorials are very rare. The majority of students would like an increase in the time spent in tutorials and in discussion groups. One possible consequence of the lack of these is that college of education students are less interested and motivated in their work than are university students, as indicated by the fact that they spend considerably less time studying. The suggestion that these several factors may be related is strengthened by a consideration of the evidence for Scottish colleges: in them the student–staff ratio is particularly high, tutorials are even less common than in the English colleges, and students, by their own report, do markedly less private study than do English college students.

Students' and teachers' attitudes to college courses

The increasing emphasis in college courses on the personal education of students and on academic studies in particular has been mentioned. Several research investigations have been concerned with the relative value which students in colleges place on academic studies and on other aspects of college courses, and with similar evaluations made by teachers a year or two after they have left college.

Williams (1963) compared the views on this subject of students in twenty-four colleges with those of teachers who had recently left college and of more experienced teachers. Results for the three groups varied in minor respects only. Much the greatest value was placed on teaching practice and much the least value on the study of academic subjects; methods of teaching specific subjects and education were given intermediate ratings. Within the category of education, all groups placed greatest emphasis on general teaching techniques; students rated the study of aims of education and then of educational psychology as next in importance, but with increasing experience, teachers put more stress on learning about schools and their organization.

The results of several other reported investigations on these questions have all been completely consistent with those of Williams. Clark and Nisbet (1963), for example, elicited the opinions of teachers who had graduated from a Scottish college of education two years before. Again, teaching practice was considered the most valuable part of the course by most students, and especially by graduate students, and 'the principal conclusion which emerged ... was that these teachers tended to regard teacher training as essentially a matter of learning the *techniques* of teaching. Other aspects of their courses, aimed to further their general education or to foster professional insight, were often regarded as a waste of time.'

An unreported investigation by the present authors, of teachers' views one year after they had graduated from another Scottish college, produced similar results. In commenting on their courses, however, students were as critical of arrangements for teaching practice and of methods lectures as of other aspects of their instruction in the college. At least in this case, therefore, it seems important to distinguish between the relative value which the teachers attached to the different areas of study and their satisfaction with the way in which these areas of study were dealt with. Asked about serious omissions from their college course, the great majority of these teachers mentioned teaching skills which they felt they had not had the opportunity to acquire; of these the most commonly mentioned were: (1) the use of specific, especially new, methods in particular subjects; there was a strong demand for practical demonstrations of these methods being used; (2) the skills of class management, discipline and establishing satisfactory relationships with pupils; teaching practice, several commented, was too 'artificial' to help much in the acquisition of these skills; (3) skill in the use of 'group methods'; (4) skill in teaching pupils of below average ability.

The comments made by teachers who had followed one-year and three-year courses were very similar.

Effects of teacher training: acquisition of skills and knowledge

Among the effects which one might hope to find resulting from teacher training courses are increased academic and professional knowledge, changes in classroom behaviour, and modifications of attitudes towards children, teaching and education.

Few investigations have been reported on the acquisition of knowledge during training. Of these, much the most extensive was a comparative cross-sectional study by Dickson (1965) of student teachers in Britain and the U.S.A. Stratified samples were chosen in both countries, but in both a number of colleges did not co-operate, thus reducing the general validity of the results. Students in each of the three college years were given a variety of tests and questionnaires, including tests in six academic subjects and in four aspects of professional knowledge. The general trend of the results is indicated by the mean total scores for academic and professional subjects given in Table 3.

Table 3 Student Attainments in Terms of Mean Total Scores.

Category of student-teachers	Academic subjects			Professional subjects		
	1st yr	2nd yr	3rd yr	1st yr	2nd yr	3rd yr
U.S. Elementary	158	152	152	111	118	124
U.K. Elementary	163	169	166	106	113	115
U.S. Secondary	168	171	170	53[1]	59	61
U.K. Secondary	175	176	193	50	53	57

1. Professional subjects totals for secondary students are for three tests only.

There is a tendency, especially in professional subjects, for scores to increase as students proceed through college. The extent of these increases however, appears to be remarkably small, although significance tests cannot be made since no standard deviations are reported.

There is equally little evidence on changes in teaching skill and classroom behaviour. Collins (1964) matched trained and untrained graduate teachers from the same English university with respect to sex, degree subject and class of degree, and compared their experiences in the first year of teaching as reported by themselves and their headmasters. Headmasters' ratings of efficiency were significantly lower for untrained than for trained teachers, and the former were more often absent from school and absent for longer periods. The design of the study, however, prevents one from inferring that these differences were due to the effects of training.

Turner (1963) presents more convincing evidence. In a series of investigations, he and his colleagues have developed tests dealing with the solution of various types of problems in teaching specific subjects; and the scores of teachers on these tests have been shown to be related to increases in the achievements of their pupils over periods of two years. Not only was it shown that training improved the attainments of student teachers in these tests, but also that such improvements could be achieved both by methods courses and by practice teaching. While this is perhaps the clearest evidence yet available that teaching ability can be improved by training, two further results should warn us against over-generalizing: the scores of beginning teachers were significantly related to the type of training institution they had attended; and the improvements made by students on teaching practice were significantly correlated with the scores of teachers with whom they were placed.

In what respects does the classroom behaviour of student teachers change during training? In one New York college (Schueler *et al.*, 1962), fifty-four students were filmed twice soon after they started their first semester's practice teaching and twice towards the end of it. It was thus possible for a detailed classification of each student's teaching behaviour to be made. The greatest changes over the semester were increased ability to keep order, being more informative in talking to pupils, in the consciousness they showed of pupils' interests and difficulties and in the amount of pupil activity in the classroom. Little change was found in the emotional responses of the student-teachers towards their pupils, or in the amount of initiative which pupils were allowed or encouraged to show. While there was no significant variation due to the different college supervisors to whom students were allocated, the changes in their teaching behaviour varied according to the school class to which they were attached. These results may well be specific to this particular college; and evidence of this type would be needed for every particular teacher-training institution which wished to know in what respects it was having greatest effect. Research of a more extended and complex nature is needed before we can isolate and describe the experiences which do, and those which do not, help students to change their classroom behaviour in ways which are desirable.

Effects of teacher training: changes in attitudes

Much the most commonly used instrument in studying teachers' attitudes has been the Minnesota Teacher Attitude Inventory. This consists of a series of statements for each of which responses are made on a five-point scale of agreement-disagreement. The statements were initially obtained from preliminary tests where they had been found to discriminate between teachers rated by their school principals as superior and those rated as inferior in their ability to maintain 'harmonious relations' with their pupils. One weakness of the instrument is the deliberate attempt made to distinguish between 'good' and 'bad' teachers; as a result, a respondent who correctly guesses the assumptions underlying the test may fake a score very much higher than that reflecting his own views. Callis (1950) found that student-teachers' scores on the M.T.A.I. increased during the course of training, especially in the first six months. More recently, Dickson (1965) found that the mean scores of American students and British students specializing in secondary school teaching were much the same for those in the third year of college courses as for those in their first year. For British primary school teachers, however, the second and third year students scored considerably higher than did those in their first year. Evans (1967) found sharp increases during training in the scores of British graduate student teachers.

The Manchester Opinion Scales in Education (Oliver and Butcher, 1962) is an instrument less value-laden in its formulation than the M.T.A.I. Butcher (1965) and McIntyre and Morrison (1967) found fairly consistent tendencies for scores on all three scales of naturalism, radicalism and tendermindedness (see page 23) to increase during training, both in colleges and in university departments of education. In comparison, indirect evidence suggested that only scores on the T-scale increased during university undergraduate courses.

Results with both these instruments therefore indicate a general tendency for attitudes to become more progressive and liberal during training. Such trends are not, however, universal. Dickson's results with American students suggest that where scores are initially high, there is less likelihood of change. Training institutions may also differ in their effects. Thus in one of the two colleges included in Butcher's investigation, students' scores on the N and T scales increased considerably during their first year, while in the other there was no significant change on either of these scales. Similarly, for those graduate students studied by McIntyre and Morrison, the large increases in scores for those trained in a college of education were on the N and R scales, while for those whose training was concentrated in a university department the greatest changes were in the T-scale scores. Investigators using other instruments have obtained results in specific colleges of a different nature; Finlayson and Cohen (1967), for example, found that students in their second year of training were significantly more child-centred and radical in their attitudes than those in their first and those in their third years.

What is the nature of these changes in the attitudes expressed by students? Do students learn to express the opinions which their lecturers hold, without necessarily being personally convinced? How permanent are the changes in attitude? Are students' attitudes reflected in their teaching styles?

The majority of studies using either the M.T.A.I. or the Manchester scales have reported no significant correlations between supervisors' ratings of students' teaching and students' attitude scores. This may be due to the unreliability of such ratings; or behaviours which reflect the attitudes assessed by these instruments may not be judged by most supervisors as indicating teaching ability. It is also possible, however, that the majority of students have not acquired the skills necessary to allow them to teach in what they believe is a desirable way. It is noteworthy that consistently significant correlations have been reported between the M.T.A.I. scores of *experienced* teachers and ratings of their teaching made by pupils, school principals and other observers.

Almost every relevant investigation, whatever the instrument used, has found that the changes in expressed attitudes during training are followed by changes in the opposite direction during the first year of teaching. For three-year trained students this reversal far from cancels out all the changes of the training period, but in the case of one-year trained graduates, Morrison and McIntyre (1967) found that the overall effect was of no significant change by the end of the two year period.

One explanation of these changes in attitude with their

subsequent reversal may lie in the influence of different social groups on the beginning teacher. The attitudes of individuals tend to change in the direction of those held by the majority in groups of which they are members, and also towards the attitudes held by groups to whose membership they aspire. Finlayson and Cohen found a considerable gap between the attitudes held by college lecturers and those held by school headmasters on many aspects of the teacher's job. They argue that the students they studied formulated their attitudes in their first two years in college within the frame of reference provided by the college, particularly its staff, but that in their final year the students were thinking more within the frame of reference used by those who would be in authority over them in the near future. Shipman (1967) similarly showed that the expressed attitudes of teachers changed in their first six months of teaching from being similar to those expressed by college staff to become much closer to those expressed by the majority of teachers in the types of school in which they were teaching.

Whatever the cause of these attitude changes, there can be no doubt that the direction of change in educational attitudes fostered by most colleges is away from, rather than towards, those which are dominant within the teaching profession as a whole; in so far as colleges are successful in modifying students' attitudes, much of this success is short lived. Shipman goes further and suggests that the attitude changes revealed by attitude scales and questionnaires during training only reflect the students' growing awareness of the 'right answers' expected of them. Meanwhile they reveal in less formal ways attitudes which are more akin to and more influenced by those of the teachers with whom they come into contact during teaching practice. Whether or not this is the case, so long as training is conceived as an initial once-and-for-all experience before entering the teaching profession, and so long as college lecturers are perceived as being separate and distinct from the body of practising teachers, it seems unlikely that they can exert an influence over young teachers comparable to that of experienced colleagues within the schools.

Another pressure towards attitude reversal, however, may arise from the experiences of beginning teachers within their own classrooms. One might perhaps say that, when faced with the practical problems of teaching, experience quickly 'obliges' them to adopt more 'realistic' views of what types of teaching behaviour are most desirable. More precisely, they may find that in order to keep control, they are behaving in ways which are contrary to the attitudes they hold, and in attempting to reduce this mental conflict they find it easier to modify their attitudes than to change their behaviour. Such a formulation is well in accord with accounts of their early experiences given by many teachers. If this is the case, it would seem that teacher-training institutions can only be effective propagandists for progressive education in so far as they can teach their students the skills required for progressive teaching.

Overview

Those who enter upon teaching careers might have distinctive characteristics and skills either as a result of formal and informal processes of selection or as a result of their professional training.

So far as selection is concerned, there is little evidence to suggest that those who choose, or are chosen, to become teachers are other than representative of the population as a whole in their needs, attitudes or other personality traits. The characteristics of recruits to the teaching profession which seem most clearly to distinguish them as a group from the wider population are rather their educational qualifications, their social class background and their sex. Thus in determining whether he becomes a teacher an individual's personality seems to be of less importance than the social position which he occupies.

None the less, researchers have persistently assumed that it is possible to provide a scientific foundation for guidance and selection procedures by identifying personality characteristics associated with 'successful' or 'effective' teaching. Their efforts, however, have met with almost universal failure; nor is there much hope for progress in this direction until a more analytic view of the activities of teachers is taken, until criteria are defined in terms of such analyses, and until much more reliable methods of observation and assessment are used.

Largely because of the lack of adequate assessment instruments, little is known about the effects of professional training on teaching behaviour. Apart from the general finding that students' educational attitudes are at least temporarily changed by their training, any belief about the value of teacher training must still depend very largely on the subjective impressions of individuals. Where evidence on the effects of training is so sparse, argument about the relative merits of different types of courses must be necessarily concerned mainly with the choice of goals and with the theoretical basis of each course. With regard to the former, it appears that a widely held opinion among students and practising teachers is that colleges and departments of education place too great an emphasis on academic and theoretical studies, and that more importance should be given to the skills required by teachers in the classroom. With regard to the latter, we have argued that a major weakness of most training courses is the absence of an adequate conceptual analysis of teaching. The availability of such an analysis could allow practical training to be more systematically planned in terms of several clearly defined and differentiated goals; and, if it provided the framework for their professional studies, it could help students to relate the various facts, theories and suggestions with which they are confronted to their own classroom experiences.

Discussion of several of the major topics dealt with in this chapter appears to lead to the same general conclusion:

little progress in either the selection or training of teachers is possible without extensive research into the classroom behaviour of teachers and their pupils, and particularly into the relation of different patterns of classroom inter-action to the achievement of long-term and intermediate educational objectives. Only with such research may it be possible to identify any personal characteristics of teachers which are related to success in particular aspects of teaching, or to identify those skills in which it is most necessary for student-teachers to be trained.

3   Teachers' Roles and Relationships

The processes of selection and training will determine who become teachers and how, to some extent, they approach their work. But a third and very significant influence is that of the schools in which they teach and of the various people who, in different ways, are associated with the schools.

Many aspects of a teacher's role are shaped by the society, or the community in which he works. Those relationships with other members of the community which are particularly significant for him vary according to cultural, geographical and administrative features of the context in which he is teaching. For example, a private tutor, a teacher who is the only teacher in a small rural community, and a teacher in a large city school have different role-sets from one another, and their relationships with members of their role-sets are likely to be very different. Any detailed discussion of the interpersonal behaviour affecting teachers must therefore be limited in its generality of application. The discussion which follows is relevant to the roles and relationships of teachers working in the contexts which have been prevalent in the United Kingdom and, in some respects, in North America in recent years.

Among the people with whom most teachers have professional relationships, several groups may be distinguished, which potentially have a considerable influence upon the role of the teacher. These groups, probably the most important of which are indicated in Figure 6, communicate with the teacher in different ways and to different degrees. In the classroom, the teacher is in direct contact over extended periods with his own pupils. Beyond the classroom, there are other people within the school with whom the teacher normally has some direct contact, but who may also have considerable indirect influence upon him. Finally, the teacher's contacts with groups and individuals beyond the school tend to be occasional and tenuous; but they too may exert powerful influences on him in indirect ways.

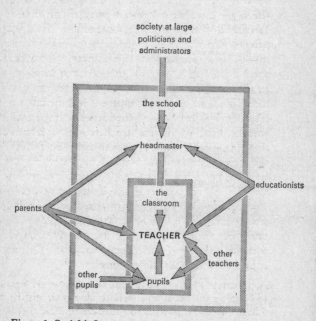

Figure 6. Social influences upon the teacher

Society Beyond the School

Parent–teacher relationships

Evidence has accumulated in recent years (e.g. Douglas, 1964) to show that the attitudes of parents towards their children's education is one of the factors most closely associated with the relative school achievements of pupils.

Among the attitudes which such studies indicate to be most influential are parents' aspirations for their children's education, as indicated by the type and length of formal education they desire for their children, and their interest in their children's education, often assessed by the number of their visits to the school. These results should however, be interpreted in the context of the type of relationships which are established between parents and teachers. As Jackson and Marsden (1962) have vividly demonstrated, parents who care greatly about their children's success may be very ignorant about the educational opportunities open to them, and too ready to accept the decisions made by teachers as the unquestionable verdict of experts. Both their ignorance and their apparent lack of interest may result from a lack of self-confidence in communicating with teachers, a belief that teachers are not interested in them or their children, or a sense that effective communication is impossible within the sort of opportunities provided by the schools. In the Plowden Committee's investigation, *Children and their Primary Schools*, the parents of a representative sample of primary school pupils in England and Wales were interviewed. While few of these parents criticized the arrangements made for them to see the teachers, they were much more critical of what normally happened when they did see them.

Approximately half of the parents said they would have liked to be told more about how their children were getting on at school. Almost a third thought that the teachers should have asked them more about their children. A fifth considered that if they went up to the school the teachers only told them what they knew already. Each of these points tended to be made more frequently by parents in the manual than non-manual occupations, suggesting that satisfactory communication between parent and teacher is considerably easier for the latter category of parents (*Children and their Primary Schools*, vol. 2, p. 131).

This is no doubt one of the factors behind the finding that 'the frequency with which parents discussed their children with the school staff ... was markedly associated with social class.'

Most parent–teacher contact in urban areas is inevitably on occasions deliberately planned for this purpose by the schools. This is especially the case where the majority of pupils are children of manual workers, since teachers are likely to live in other areas and to have few friends or pastimes in common with their pupils' parents. Open days or evenings are the most common and generally the most valued occasions for such contact. But their relative rarity in most schools, the teacher-parent ratio, and the classroom context of the meeting – with its not so pleasant associations for many parents – all combine to make most of these meetings impersonal, stereotyped and therefore of low communication value. The rather less formal contacts which are possible in parent–teacher associations appear to be greatly valued in some countries. In Britain, however, only a minority of schools have such associations, and where they exist, they appear to be largely middle-class institutions. According to the Plowden Report, 20 per cent of non-manual worker parents had been to meetings of such associations as opposed to only 5 per cent of manual workers. What most parents seem to want is effective communication between themselves and individual teachers about their individual children, rather than to acquire a general understanding of modern methods of teaching or school organization.

One way in which parent–teacher communication could be improved would be for teachers to develop more intimate and less formal relationships with parents. As interviews in the course of research have suggested, parents 'on their own ground' and in relatively informal circumstances tend to talk much more freely about their aspirations and fears for their children's future, and to reveal gaps in their knowledge of the educational system and the often inadequately formulated questions and problems it raises for them. Cohen (1967) found little enthusiasm among headmasters or student-teachers for such an extension of the teacher's role beyond the classroom. In another investigation, in a Scottish city, only one of over a hundred headmasters showed even mild approval of the suggestion that teachers might visit the homes of their pupils, the majority being definitely opposed to the idea. Certainly, if teachers were to make a serious attempt to develop closer relations with individual parents, their use of time would have to be radically revised, and a new dimension in their professional training would need to be added; but, in view of the demonstrated influence which parental attitudes have on teachers' effectiveness, such steps might be warranted.

In the apparently prevailing conditions of poor communications between parents and teachers, what norms do parents hold for teachers' behaviour and how clearly do teachers perceive these? Results of research in the United States, where such communication is generally assumed to be greater than in Britain, suggest that misconceptions may be common. Jenkins and Lippitt (1951), in a detailed study of one Massachusetts junior high school, found that teachers commonly believed that parents wished them to help their children with their personal problems, and to give them distinctive treatment; but parents rarely mentioned any desire for teachers to do these things. Biddle, Rosencranz and Rankin (1961), on the other hand, found that parents in their Mid-West sample perceived teachers as desiring to avoid participation in P.T.A.s and wishing to assert publicly their educational opinions, whereas teachers claimed that they neither wished to, nor actually did, behave in these ways.

In one of the very few British investigations in this area (Musgrove and Taylor, 1965), parents and teachers were asked to list six possible aims in order of their centrality to the teacher's role; and teachers were also asked to rank them in order of the value they believed parents placed upon them. Parents and teachers showed a high degree of agreement in giving precedence to instruction in subjects and moral training as the two most important aspects of the teacher's role, and in considering that education for family life should not be a responsibility of the teacher. But teachers greatly underestimated the importance attached by parents to the moral training and education for citizenship aspects of their role, and correspondingly exaggerated the emphasis which parents placed on the teacher's role as an agent of social advancement for pupils. They perceived parents as expecting them to treat social advancement as second only in importance to instruction; in fact, parents tended to rank this as the second least important of the six aims.

Musgrove and Taylor's comment that 'on the whole, teachers take an unflattering view of parents' is hardly justified by their evidence, since equality of opportunity for social advancement is one of the widely applauded official virtues of the British educational system, and it might well be considered that moral training is the responsibility of the home rather than that of the school; but its validity is borne out by less systematic evidence from other sources. They conclude that 'the area of (unnecessary) tension might be considerably reduced, if parents and teachers established more effective means of communication'. However, while better communication would no doubt decrease teachers' misconceptions, the assumption that this perceived disagreement with parents *is* an area of tension for teachers has yet to be verified. The evidence that teachers tend to have a poor opinion of the attitudes of most parents, and that they do not show any great concern to establish more effective communication with them, suggests rather that teachers do not feel the need to pay much attention to parents' opinions; but no direct evidence is available on this.

There are many unanswered questions with regard to the relation between parental attitudes and behaviour and the work of schools. We do not know, for example, what accounts for the statistical relationship between parental attitudes and pupil achievements. To what extent is it explained by the differential behaviour of teachers towards pupils from different home backgrounds? Nor do we know what the effects of better communication between parents and teachers would be. In the Plowden Committee's investigation, the average attainments of pupils in a group of schools selected by inspectors as having particularly good parent–teacher relations were not found to be significantly different from those of pupils in the representative sample of schools. Whether the attitudes of teachers, parents or neither would change no doubt depends on both the nature and the direction of the communication. Parents appear to want both to hear things from teachers and to tell them things. Do teachers want to listen as well as to tell? Perhaps the most fundamental gap in our knowledge is of the types of behaviour commonly exhibited by parents and teachers towards one another when they do meet.

The teacher and educational 'experts'

There are several groups of people beyond the school, apart from administrators, who are professionally concerned with school education. Among these are college of education lecturers, school inspectors and educational researchers.

As indicated in the previous chapter, many teachers consider that their initial training was not sufficiently aimed at giving them a mastery of the practical skills required for classroom teaching, and that the educational principles propounded were not sufficiently realistic. Most contacts between serving teachers and the staff of colleges are in the context of in-service training courses. As yet, nearly all such courses are optional for British teachers and are arranged at times which do not conflict with their teaching. They are therefore run on a supply and demand basis, and it is noteworthy that the great majority of these courses are concerned with such 'hard' material as new techniques of instruction like audiovisual aids and new subject content. Courses on subjects like classroom management, motivation and discipline, communication or teacher–parent relations are rare. Whereas in pre-service training lecturers can impose on their students what they think they ought to know, the relationship is almost reversed in in-service training: college lecturers are only given the opportunity to discuss those 'useful' subjects about which teachers want to be informed.

The role of the inspector is an ambiguous one. As an experienced teacher himself, he is expected to advise younger teachers on how they can improve their teaching. He is also expected, by reading and attending conferences, but mainly by visiting a variety of schools, to be informed on educational innovations, to assess these, and to keep teachers informed about them. In addition to these functions as adviser, critic and reporter, however, he is also an assessor who has power over teachers. Central government inspectors are responsible for ensuring that local authorities and their employees are carrying out their duties efficiently and in accordance with the law, and for judging whether probationer teachers are sufficiently competent to become fully accredited members of the profession. Local authority inspectors can often determine which teachers are to receive promotion. While there are probably few teachers who witness the approach of an inspector without some anxiety, virtually nothing is known about the influence which inspectors have on the behaviour of teachers. The potential influence of central government inspectors is probably limited by the length of time which commonly elapses between their visits to any one school, and it may be that local inspectors, who can visit their schools regularly, are more influential. The combination of the power which they can have over teachers and their opportunity to be better informed than most teachers puts them in a position to exert considerable pressure.

In general, teachers are very little influenced by educational research and place little value upon it. Johnson (1966) found that few teachers attempted to keep themselves informed of the results of research, but that those who were most knowledgeable about research results and those who did most reading related to their professional work placed significantly more value upon research than did others. Having been involved in or associated with a research project in the past was another factor which inclined teachers to a more favourable attitude towards research. Johnson also found that there was a high correlation between the attitudes of the headmaster to research and those of his staff.

Among probable reasons for indifference or antipathy towards research are that most teachers have received no training in the assessment of research or the use of its results; that it is not easy to change one's teaching practices in accordance with the conclusions of research, as a doctor can prescribe a new drug; and that few research results up to the present have straightforward and immediate implications for teaching. Other reasons are the organizational and therefore often the social distance between teachers and researchers. British schools are not, as in some countries, organized with facilities for research 'built in', so that every research project causes a disruption of the work of one or more teachers. This, together with teachers' lack of enthusiasm, unfortunately tends to encourage researchers to engage in projects which will have the least disruptive effect upon the schools – and hence to avoid those projects which might provide the most useful and stimulating insights for teachers.

Relations Within the School

Schools, like other institutions, tend to have their own distinctive 'atmosphere'. Some 'feel' more friendly than others, some more efficient, and some more alive with enthusiasm and activity. Although there are inevitably wide variations in the personalities and behaviour of the people in any school, the complex network of social relations and the regularly recurring interaction between different individuals and groups create conditions in which the behaviour of all the people in the school can become closely interdependent. In particular, those in positions of formal authority, such as the headmaster, and those who emerge as leading members of informal groups of teachers or pupils can have an extensive influence on the patterns of behaviour which develop and on the behavioural norms of the school community.

A teacher's relations with his pupils are of pre-eminent importance, but these relationships are formed within the context of the wider social unit of the school and there are several aspects of a teacher's experiences within, and attitudes towards, this wider unit, which may affect his teaching behaviour. Among these are:

1. Relations with the headmaster and others in authority.
2. Informal relations with other teachers.
3. Conceptions of the appropriate goals for the particular 'type' of school.
4. The social organization of the school; in particular, the formal grouping of pupils for teaching purposes.

The headmaster

Headmasters in British schools are men with great power, and in consequence the social climate of a school depends much more on their behaviour than on that of other individuals. Usually given considerable freedom by local authorities and governing bodies, they are in positions of complete authority within the law over everyone else in their schools. In addition, by having a good deal of control over the appointment of teachers to better paid jobs, they can exert strong financial pressure on teachers.

The role of the headmaster is extremely vague. Since, almost without exception, headmasters are experienced teachers, one might assume that their prime responsibility was to supervise teaching in the school, and to advise less experienced teachers on how they can improve their teaching. Yet few headmasters seem to spend much of their time observing teachers at work. In many schools, the facet of the job most obvious to the school population as a whole is that of 'last ditch' disciplinarian. No special

training in other possible aspects of the role, such as coun-
selling, administration and management, curriculum development, social welfare work and public relations is normally
available in Britain.

Because headmasters are officially responsible for every-
thing that happens within their schools, they may feel
obliged to stress those aspects of school activities which
are most visible to those outside. Success in external
examinations, 'respectable' dress and hairstyles of pupils,
efficient completion of forms for the central office, school
concerts and plays, special projects for open days, and
successful sports teams are some of these aspects. Headmasters who expect their teachers to produce appropriate
results in these ways can be a source of role-conflict for
teachers. Partridge (1967) has documented the way in
which one headmaster's concern for some of these activities
had a seriously disruptive effect on teaching in the school.
Whether the majority of headmasters in this country do
emphasize such things is unknown, as are other aspects
of their behaviour. The new teacher in a school can be sure
of only one thing about the headmaster: that he is 'the
boss'. He cannot know what demands the headmaster will
make of him, nor what assistance and support he can expect
from him. Since both teacher and head will, however,
have expectations of the other's behaviour towards him
derived from their previous experiences, this lack of definition of the headmaster's role is a potential source of considerable misunderstanding and tension.

In large schools, some of the headmaster's work is
delegated to a deputy head; and in secondary schools,
heads of departments and in some cases housemasters
are also figures in the authority structure. The existence of
these intermediaries can lead to headmasters having very
little contact with many of the teachers in their schools
and to indirect communication between the head and
teachers. In such circumstances, those in the peripheral
positions in the communication network may feel dissatisfied both with the system as a whole and with their

own place in it; not only are assistant teachers likely to receive partial and imperfect information about the policies of the school, but their involvement in their own work is also likely to be affected by their position in the authority hierarchy. Kelley (1951) found that in experimentally created groups in which members were given high or low status, the number of communications irrelevant to the task of the groups were significantly greater among the low-status members. Similarly, in a study of communication among teachers in an American high school, it was found that while most of the conversation between teachers was about school policy matters, assistant teachers who were recent recruits to the school talked least about these and spent much more time than senior members of the staff discussing personal matters which had nothing to do with the work of the school. It would seem that where the communication network conforms to the formal authority structure, much of the energy which teachers could give to their professional concerns is diverted into other channels.

Headmasters are sometimes referred to as leaders of the staff of their schools. 'Leadership' is an ambiguous concept, and it has been defined in many ways. Two characteristics of leaders about which there is fairly general agreement, however, are that the leader of a group is a member of the group, and that he exerts more influence on the group than any other member. By this definition, it is clear that headmasters may or may not be leaders; for example, a headmaster who rarely talks with most of his staff cannot be considered a member of the staff group or therefore its leader. One may ask both what the effects of a headmaster acting as a leader are, and what different sorts of leadership may be used.

The most extensive study which has been carried out of the behaviour of headmasters is the National Principalship Study (Gross and Herriot, 1965) in which a representative sample of principals in cities in the United States were given lengthy interviews, and questionnaires were completed by members of their staff. Assessments were made of the extent to which principals gave their staff 'professional leadership', characterized by such behaviour as placing obvious importance on meetings with their staff, giving advice to teachers, and attempting to achieve a high level of staff motivation. This professional leadership was distinguished from the principals' efficiency as administrators. It was found that in schools where principals gave more professional leadership, ratings of teachers' classroom performances, the assessed attainments of pupils, and ratings of teachers' morale were all higher than in schools where such leadership was less apparent. Principals rated high on leadership also tended to have more democratic relations with their staffs. Among other variables associated with leadership, it was found to be negatively correlated with the amount of training in educational administration which principals had undergone; it is perhaps more likely that this is a reflection of the personality characteristics of principals who are particularly concerned with the administrative aspects of their role than that courses in administration themselves have a deleterious effect.

The behaviour of headmasters and others in authority in education appears to vary in two main aspects of leadership. Halpin (1956) found that the behaviour of school superintendents can be analysed as varying along two dimensions, which he labelled as Initiating Structure and Consideration. The former refers to a leader's behaviour in organizing the group, in establishing, for example, the functions of different members; the latter refers to behaviour showing trust, warmth and respect in relationships with members of his staff. Other investigations have shown that two similar dimensions may be useful in describing the ways in which schools are organized. Getzels and Guba (1957) distinguished three idealized types of leader, the nomothetic, the ideographic and the transactional. The nomothetic leader stresses the requirements of the institution and its functions, places importance on conformity with general rules and with his expectations, and judges members of the staff group in terms of their effectiveness. The ideographic leader makes few organizational demands, places most importance on the individual needs of members of the staff, seeks personal relationships with each of them suited to these needs and relies heavily upon teachers' own values to ensure that their work is done adequately. In Getzels' view, the leader likely to be most effective is the transactional leader, that is one who shows a balanced and flexible concern for both the needs of the individual members and the tasks of the institution. In Halpin's terminology, the transactional leader is high on both initiating structure and consideration. Guba and Bidwell (1957) found that teachers' perceptions of the extent to which their principals gave transactional leadership was significantly correlated with the teachers' assessments of their own satisfaction and effectiveness.

One of the difficulties of research in this area is that it is not easy to obtain a reliable record of a headmaster's behaviour over a long enough period. Most investigations have in fact relied upon the reports of principals about their own behaviour or on the reports of others thought to be in positions to make assessments. Typically it has been found that reports and assessments vary considerably according to their source. In the research of Guba and Bidwell mentioned above, for example, the significant correlations found were between variables all of which were obtained from the responses of the same people; the principals' own reports of their leadership behaviour, however, were unrelated to the self-assessments of teachers. Apart from the research problems which the unreliability of such evidence causes, it also emphasizes the centrality of social interaction in the principal's role: his effectiveness depends not only upon his behaviour, but upon how the behaviour affects and is perceived by the teachers and others with whom he works.

Informal relations among teachers

In their investigation of the sources of dissatisfaction among a large and 'not unrepresentative' group of teachers five years after they completed training, Rudd and Wiseman (1962) found that 'poor human relations among the school staff' was a source of complaint second only to salaries in its frequency. Although such relationships are then clearly important to many teachers, little is known about them; the factors which determine the formation of social groups among teachers, the channels of communication which are developed, the nature and extent of group pressures upon individual teachers, and the types of interpersonal conflicts which arise, are all at present largely unexplored. One of the reasons for this lack of evidence is undoubtedly the reluctance of teachers for such 'private' concerns to be treated as a subject for research. Hargreaves (1967), reporting his very revealing study of social relations in one school, felt obliged to omit references to relations among teachers since information about these was confidential.

The social groups which are formed among the teachers in a school can be partly the result of the school organization. In secondary schools, the departmental organization of teaching generally brings those with the same specialist subject into greater contact with one another than with other teachers. Staffroom accommodation can also be an important factor. Where all the staff share a common room, it is relatively easy for individuals to seek out and form friendships with others who share their values and interests. Where both staffrooms and teaching departments are situated in different parts of the school buildings, the tendency for groups to be department-based is strongly reinforced; and where separate staffrooms are provided for men and women, the possibility that there will be social groups with members of both sexes is greatly decreased. Other factors which may be important in the formation of groups are age, teaching experience and experience within the particular school. These are also factors which often determine status within groups. Partridge (1967), for example, noted that 'in the course of dinner-time discussions, the stories, jokes and topics of conversation are usually decided by the senior teachers. Seldom does a junior member initiate conversation or voice strong opinions other than or contrary to those of his seniors'.

In primary schools in particular, it seems likely that age, sex and marital status are important determinants of social groups. Married women who have entered or returned to teaching after raising their families increasingly form sizeable minorities with common interests. Men, who tend to be dominant in both numbers and status in secondary schools, form a minority group in primary schools who, according to Rudd and Wiseman's data, are more dissatisfied than other teachers; it is probably common for them to form social sub-groups. Young teachers who have recently left college, if they want the satisfaction and support to be gained from acceptance by their colleagues must commonly aspire to membership of groups of relatively experienced teachers. But where such young teachers find a sizeable minority of others in their own position, they may often find their company more pleasant and less demanding; and this is a situation which occurs more frequently in primary than in secondary schools.

The social relations among teachers in a school, and particularly the formation of informal groups among them, are relevant to the work of the school in at least two respects. Firstly, the pressure from a group for its members to conform to group norms is likely to influence their teaching behaviour and their relationships with pupils. Secondly, there may be in a school a high degree of consensus among teachers or there may be conflicts between different groups: this too can have important repercussions in the classroom.

As was shown in the previous chapter, students tend to become more 'progressive' in their educational attitudes during their professional training; but, having completed their training, they tend in their first years of teaching to change their attitudes in the direction of those held by other teachers in their schools, which usually means adopting less progressive attitudes. One of the factors accounting for this reversal of attitude change is doubtless that, encountering as they do similar experiences in their teaching to those of teachers in the same school, they tend similarly to acquire the attitudes which enable them most easily to cope with these experiences. Complementary to this influence of the young teacher's classroom experience, however, is the direct influence of other teachers.

Extensive laboratory research has established many of the factors which induce people to conform to the behaviour of a group. A person is more likely to accept the group's judgement than his own when the problem is difficult, when the other members of the group form a friendship group into which he would like to be accepted, and when he perceives the other members as having greater expertise than himself. All these conditions are likely to be applicable to the situation of a newly qualified teacher among more experienced teachers in a school. Considering the evidence mentioned earlier that those who become teachers tend to be more prone than average to conforming behaviour, it is clear that the more experienced members of staff can often greatly influence the novice to conform to their views.

Almost certainly the most common source of conflict among teachers is 'discipline', which is understandable since it is this aspect of each teacher's work which has greatest and most immediate effect upon the work of his colleagues. The degree to which a maths teacher is successful in giving his pupils an understanding of his subject is virtually irrelevant to the task of those who teach these pupils French or geography. But the authoritarian teacher and the teacher who encourages pupils to be friendly and outspoken in his class each presents a very clear threat to the other's chances of establishing his desired relationship with pupils. In addition, a class which is uncontrolled and noisy can disturb the concentration of other classes and 'give them ideas'. Conflict over discipline, however, probably goes deeper than this. As Musgrove and Taylor (1965) have shown, the majority of teachers consider the moral training of children to be an important aspect of their teaching role. One implication of this is that they themselves hold moral codes with sufficient confidence to impose them on their pupils. In such circumstances, a teacher who, by his tolerance of pupils' behaviour, 'encourages moral laxity', and one who, by his use of corporal punishment, 'encourages the use of violence' are likely to regard one another not simply as incompetent, but as immoral in their behaviour towards pupils.

Other sources of conflict among the teachers in a school can be the threat which one teacher or department is perceived to offer to the status of another teacher or department; a belief that some members of staff are not given a fair share of the school's work or are not fully accepting their responsibilities (extramural activities and dinner and playground duty being common sources of such conflict); a belief held by teachers of certain subjects, such as physical education and technical subjects, that other members of staff undervalue their contribution to the work of the school; and jealousy over favouritism which some teachers are thought to receive from the headmaster, for example in being timetabled for 'easy' classes.

Recent American research indicates that the extent to which there is consensus among the staff of a school depends very much on the policies and behaviour of the principal, especially in the amount of person-oriented (ideographic) leadership he offers. The principal is also one of the people who has most to lose from conflict among the staff, for it then becomes difficult for him to get co-operation in the carrying out of school policies and in particular to achieve a general acceptance of any proposed changes. However, those for whom the results of staff conflict can be most serious are the pupils, especially when they are used in it. They can be used as a source of information, being invited to make comments about what happens in other teachers' classes; as a teacher's property, not available to other teachers; as status symbols, being required to reflect in their behaviour and attainments their teacher's ability; or even as weapons, being encouraged to behave in ways which are calculated to disturb or inconvenience other teachers. While systematic research would be necessary to understand the various ways in which staff conflict can affect pupils, subjective impressions of schools in which it has occurred suggest that their motivation, their enjoyment of life and work in the school and their acceptance of the authority of teachers can be markedly decreased by their perception of staff conflict; and that the status and influence of pupils least inclined to cooperate with teachers tends to increase in such situations.

Type of school

Schools can be classified in innumerable ways, but from the viewpoint of social psychology two of the most fundamental are (a) their purposes as conceived by those associated with them, and (b) the characteristics and social backgrounds of pupils attending them. In Britain, these two bases of classification are closely interrelated, especially when applied to secondary schools. The differences among secondary modern, grammar, comprehensive and independent schools reflect both these aspects. In particular, grammar school and secondary modern school pupils tend to differ in their social class backgrounds, and, as will be demonstrated, teachers within them tend to have correspondingly different educational and social purposes. It is therefore difficult, and perhaps misleading, to distinguish between the effects of institutional traditions and of pupil characteristics upon the attitudes and purposes of teachers in different schools.

Musgrove and Taylor (1965) found significant differences between modern and grammar school teachers in the importance they attached to several suggested aims of teaching. Grammar school teachers were more inclined to categorize some purposes as 'no concern of mine', and tended to give a higher priority to instruction. Modern school teachers were on the whole more concerned than those in grammar schools with social training and, among the men, with moral training. These differences were minor shifts of emphasis within what at first appears to be a common framework of priorities: teachers in both types of school most often rated instruction and moral training as their two most important aims. Such blanket phrases, however, can hide important qualitive differences.

In her study of 'the social and educational assumptions of the grammar school', Stevens (1960) elicited the views of English grammar school teachers in nineteen schools which were varied in size, sex composition and geographical location. One significant feature of the statements made by many of the teachers is that they clearly did not conceive of academic instruction and moral training as *separate* aspects of their role. A recurring theme is of the 'civilizing' influence of grammar school study: 'to protect as far as possible ... the culture of European civilization', 'to give an introduction to the humanities and a training in intellectual processes, and thus provide a healthy counterbalance to the influence of the cinema, I.T.A. and Radio Luxembourg ...', 'to produce a generation of pupils who have a clear conception of the correct set of Christian standards and values and who have been trained to think for themselves ...'. Such statements of aims assume that for teachers to concern themselves primarily with the knowledge and quality of thinking of their pupils is also automatically to influence their pupils towards certain tastes, moral values and patterns of living. Similarly, the grammar school should aim to inculcate those virtues which are often summed up in the word 'character', and the most important and effective way in which character is to be 'built' is by requiring pupils to work hard at their academic studies. The majority of these teachers thought that pupils would gain something from the discipline of studying their subject, even when they did not understand the work.

A second attitude revealed in the teachers' statements is that the ideals represented by grammar schools are under attack by powerful forces in the rest of society. A grammar school community is therefore a minority élite which must be protected from undesirable influences from without. School uniform, in the words of one teacher, should be used as 'a symbol, a reminder that each wearer of it is a member of a very special community'. This sense of exclusiveness extended to the activities thought appropriate for pupils outside school, shown for example in attitudes to youth clubs. Some teachers were concerned lest other activities might interfere with pupils' studies, or considered that 'youth clubs should not interest the grammar school girl, who is amply provided for at school and at home in social and cultural development'. Others were concerned rather with social exclusiveness: 'I doubt if there is much value in meeting children from another intellectual class, such as are found in youth clubs. It would be easy to drop to their level of activity'.

Commonly mentioned goals for the grammar school were the training of pupils in leadership and a willingness to serve the community, though this could, for some teachers, conflict with the desired social exclusiveness of the school. One aspect of this preparation of future leaders for society was equipping pupils with the knowledge and skills required to gain, and to carry out, 'responsible' jobs, particularly in the professions. While there was virtually universal rejection of the idea that grammar school education should be solely concerned with vocational aims or with the acquisition of formal qualifications, many admitted that in practice their over-riding aim was the achievement of maximum success in G.C.E. examinations. And, although some believed that they would do a more effective job in the absence of external exams, the fact that these provided the immediate 'goal and justification of most school effort' did not appear to conflict greatly with the more long-term purposes of the teachers.

One further aspect of the teachers' attitudes revealed by Stevens' data is that many of the goals which they considered grammar schools should pursue and many aspects of the way of life within these schools were dependent on assumptions made about the attributes of pupils and of their homes. Grammar school pupils should have acquired proper manners and morals at home; they should be hard-working and keen to succeed; parents should accept and support the authority of the school on educational matters; and they should ensure that their children's leisure activities are appropriate and do not interfere with their school work. That teachers commonly found that such assumptions were 'nowadays' unjustified was a source of much frustration.

The picture which has been presented of the attitudes of grammar school teachers gives no indication of the variations which undoubtedly exist among schools and among teachers. There are good reasons to believe, however, that there is much greater uniformity among grammar schools in the goals their teachers pursue than there is among other secondary schools in this country. Secondary modern schools neither have the guiding (and inhibiting) influence of a national tradition which has developed over centuries, nor, generally, the dominating pressure of external examinations for the majority of their pupils. According to the Newsom Report, 'the very absence of a set pattern has attracted men and women with a zest for pioneering. As a result, the schools are growing up – for the process is still going on – very varied in character' (Half Our Future, p. 12).

The most confident generalization one can make about the aims and assumptions of teachers in secondary modern schools is that they are not the same as those of grammar school teachers: their schools are not exclusive communities, they are not training leaders or scholars, and they do not see their pupils as the potential guardians of the culture of European civilization. Oliver and Butcher (1968) found that teachers in secondary modern schools had significantly more naturalistic attitudes to education than grammar school teachers, i.e. they saw education more as a process of individual development and less as one of the preparation of pupils for defined goals. So far as academic education is concerned, schools vary from those which, like the grammar schools, place heavy emphasis on success in external examinations for as many pupils as possible to those like one described by Hargreaves (1967), where 'for many of the teachers and most of the pupils, life at school was a necessary evil. Life was directed towards a reduction of potential conflict by a minimal imposition of demands upon one another. If the upper streams passed their examinations and the lower streams did not riot, the school was, for most teachers, succeeding.' The recurring mention in several first-hand accounts of these schools of such lack of pressure for achievement suggests that it is quite common; it implies that, with some pupils at least, teachers have 'given up', and have no goals of a cognitive nature at all. Beyond this continuum from much to little academic pressure, there are schools in which goals are conceived in terms of the interests of pupils and of the concrete realities of their present and future lives, rather than in terms of distinct school subjects; but neither the scale of such reformulations of goals nor the ways in which they are interpreted by individual teachers is clear.

The evidence of Musgrove and Taylor, however, suggested that the emphasis in secondary modern schools on moral and social training is of even greater importance than that given to these aims in grammar schools. Some indication of the nature of these aims is given by an investigation in Scotland carried out by Craig (1960). By interviews and group discussions, Craig attempted to establish the conceptions of their roles held by volunteer groups of teachers in senior and junior secondary schools (the Scottish equivalents of grammar and modern schools respectively). He found that senior secondary teachers were 'preoccupied with the development of the intellectual faculties'; like the teachers in Stevens' sample, however, they thought of such intellectual instruction as having implicit within it an inculcation of desirable moral values and a training for citizenship. 'Training for citizenship' was an aim to which junior secondary teachers attached a more direct importance, but with a rather different meaning. They commonly perceived in their pupils either a lack of moral values or wrong values, and attributing these moral inadequacies to the undesirable influence of the pupils' home backgrounds, set themselves the task of filling the gap left by, or counteracting the influence of, the homes. Thus, whereas the aims of grammar and senior secondary teachers are predetermined and depend for their realization upon the validity of several exacting assumptions about the home backgrounds of pupils, those of junior secondary teachers appear to be much less related to preconceived goals, but rather to be a response to a perceived lack of desirable values in the social classes from which most of their pupils come. Craig noted that senior secondary teachers also perceived a lack of moral values in their younger pupils, but ascribed this to their immaturity.

In a selective system, the educational goals of teachers thus appear to be closely related to the different socio-economic functions the two types of school are conceived to have and to be dependent upon stereotyped beliefs about the pupils who attend them. In future, secondary schools in Britain are to be comprehensive. That the pupils in such schools cannot as a group be assumed to have any distinctive characteristics except their age (and perhaps the district in which they live) may lessen the effects of teachers' preconceptions. Such evidence as is available indicates that on the whole comprehensive schools promote greater cultural and social unity among pupils and make education more purposive for them, but also that there are wide variations among comprehensive schools in these respects. There is unfortunately no direct evidence about the preconceptions or the goals of teachers in British comprehensive schools.

Teachers' attitudes to their work differ according to the social class background of their schools even when the schools are administratively of the same type. In a study of the ways in which primary school teachers in a Scottish city assessed their pupils' characteristics (McIntyre *et al.*, 1966), differences were found between teachers in different areas of the city; in particular, there were variations in the pupil characteristics which teachers were found to associate with the judgement 'pupil worth taking trouble over'. Teachers in middle-class schools thought boys who were pleasant, trustworthy and generally well-behaved were most worthy of their efforts. Those in suburban working-class areas were more inclined to take trouble over boys whose attainments were highest and who showed original-ity, enthusiasm and social confidence; and those in central urban working-class districts most valued attainment together with attentiveness, co-operation with the teacher and persistence. Assessments of girls, however, stressed 'good behaviour' irrespective of the social class of the school.

As the Newsom Report, for example, revealed, staff turnover is considerably greater in schools in 'slum' districts than elsewhere. While statistical evidence (*Children and Their Primary Schools*, 1967) shows that, at least in primary schools, staff turnover is not in itself related to the average attainments of pupils in schools, the effects of the type of turnover – what sort of teachers stay, and what sort go – remain unresolved. In one interesting study in Chicago, Becker (1952) found that young teachers found the difficulties of instruction and discipline to be much greater if they were in schools in 'slum' districts. Very early, therefore, the majority sought transfer to equivalent jobs in 'better' neighbourhoods. A minority, who did not find jobs in other areas, tended to adapt themselves to working in these schools by reducing their aspirations for pupil attainment, by learning effective disciplinary techniques and by finding satisfaction in the informal prestige they held among colleagues because of their easily acquired seniority. But, having so adapted themselves, their repertoire of teaching behaviours made them misfits in schools in other areas, so encouraging them to remain in the slum schools.

A more recent study (Herriott and St John, 1966) considered the effect of pupil background upon teachers in a representative sample of schools in American cities. The schools were placed in four categories of socio-economic status on the basis of the family income, the occupation of fathers and the education of parents of the majority of pupils. In schools of lower socio-economic status, the teachers tended to be younger and less experienced, to have been in that school for a shorter time, to be less likely to wish to spend the rest of their careers in that school, and to be less satisfied with many aspects of their jobs, especially the academic performance of their pupils. All these results suggest that Becker's conclusions may be generalizable within the United States at least. A further result of this study was that in many respects teachers in schools of the lowest socio-economic status tended to enjoy the work of teaching more than those in 'better' areas. Despite this, the average competence of teachers, as assessed by colleagues and principals, was in almost all respects (e.g. interest taken in pupils, experimentation with new methods) lowest in schools of low socio-economic status. It seems surprising that teachers who appear to be less successful in their work and also to be less satisfied with their present jobs should enjoy the work of teaching more than others. The solution to this anomaly may be that the gross statistical results are an artefact resulting from the characteristics of the two main groups in slum schools described by Becker, the mobile group being more dissatisfied than average, the adaptive group enjoying teaching more than average; that this second group should not be particularly competent would be consistent with his suggestion that they have adapted themselves to their situation partly by being less demanding of themselves.

Grouping of pupils

The social environment of a teacher within a school is greatly affected by the school's policies in grouping pupils. These may affect the number and characteristics of pupils in the classes he teaches, the informal status hierarchy among the staff, and particularly through their effect upon attitudes and social relationships of pupils, the whole social climate of the school.

The range of grouping policies which are possible or usual depends upon the age-group of the pupils, upon whether the same educational goals are thought to be appropriate for them all, and upon the size of the school. Yates (1966) reviews the variety of grouping procedures which are commonly used in European and North American countries and the results of research into their relative 'effectiveness'. He concludes that 'in arguments about grouping policies one can usually find evidence to support any point of view one chooses to adopt – enough evidence to discomfit one's opponent but never enough to overwhelm him'. However, 'there is strongly suggestive evidence that grouping based on distinctions such a measured ability, membership of a social class, racial group or religious denomination helps to emphasize or even exaggerate these distinctions.'

Streaming. Much the most common type of grouping in Britain is streaming, the division of pupils into classes according to some assessment of academic ability or attainment. Although some investigations have obtained apparently conflicting results, the weight of evidence suggests that streaming does not increase the mean of children's attainments, but does increase the spread; a tentative generalization might be that it tends to depress the attainments of those in lower streams, but may in some circumstances increase those of pupils in upper streams. It may also lead to greater anxiety and poorer emotional

adjustment among pupils and to less mixing among children from different social backgrounds (e.g. Willig, 1963).
That research has so far been inconclusive is not surprising,
since little account has generally been taken of the attitudes
of teachers, a factor which appears to be crucial.

In an investigation carried out by the National Foundation for Educational Research (1967), fifty streamed primary schools, chosen at random, were compared with
fifty non-streamed schools with regard to pupils' attainments and the attitudes and characteristics of teachers.
Not only did few of the teachers disapprove of the grouping
methods used in their own schools, but significant differences between the two teacher samples were found in that
those in streamed schools tended to be less permissive
in their attitudes to children's behaviour, more in favour
of corporal punishment, and more in favour of the eleven
plus examination. They used more formal teaching methods and gave more tests, and on average they were older.
The report concludes that 'the two kinds of school seem
to embody different views about children and different
philosophies of education'. Interim results suggest that
teachers' attitudes to streaming and their associated educational philosophies are at least as important as the grouping
system actually used in affecting the attitudes of pupils
and their attainments in various subjects.

In streamed schools, the N.F.E.R. investigation found
that teachers who taught the abler streams tended to be
older and more experienced, to be more favourably dis-
posed towards streaming, to favour secondary school
selection, and to be less tolerant of noise. Jackson (1964)
similarly concluded from his detailed study of several
streamed primary schools that teachers were themselves
often streamed, those most concerned with examination
results and most demanding of hard work and obedient
behaviour being allocated to the ablest streams. Reports
from secondary schools suggest that the least experienced,
the least qualified, those with least effective control over
pupil behaviour and those who are transitory members of

staff are commonly given the lower streams to teach. While this teacher streaming is sometimes the result of a deliberate policy on the part of headmasters, it also tends to be desired by the teachers of greatest status and experience. To teach a top stream is often considered a necessary stepping-stone to promotion; and it is also commonly seen as a reward for good service, since pupil co-operation and learning is more easily achieved in the upper streams.

The existence of streaming in a school has a considerable influence on teacher–pupil relationships. Pupils are allocated to high or low streams according to the degree to which they are perceived to possess certain characteristics valued by teachers, such as academic abilities, conscientiousness, and enthusiasm for learning. Allocation to a top stream may therefore be interpreted by pupils, quite rightly, as a mark of their acceptability to teachers and as a reward for their past behaviour, and allocation to a low stream as a mark of rejection. This acceptance by teachers is likely to reinforce the good behaviour of those in the top stream and their selection as members of a high status group may encourage conformity to the standards of behaviour which give them this status; while those in the lower streams, one may expect, will tend to show hostility towards those whom they believe to be rejecting them. Because they spend most of their time at school in their streamed classes, pupils tend to form friendship groups with those in their own streams, and to mix much less with those in other streams. The influence of peer-groups thus strengthens the differential tendencies; the norms of behaviour upheld by the dominant groups in A stream classes often supplement the demands of teachers upon pupils, whereas in C, D or E streams, pupils more often tend to be exposed to conflicting demands from their peers and from their teachers.

Hargreaves (1967), in his study of social relations in Lumley Secondary Modern School, has made one of the few reported attempts to systematically investigate teacher–pupil relations in a streamed school. He shows how closely interrelated were the behaviour of teachers towards pupils, the attitudes of pupils in different streams towards the school, and the relations among pupils of the same and different streams. In the fourth year of school, most of the pupils chose their friends from within the same stream. At one extreme was 4A, whose norms for their own behaviour were almost identical with those of their teachers, and at the other 4D, antipathetic to school, to learning, and to the values of 'respectable' society. Each of these two groups rejected and despised the other, applying negative stereotypes to members of the other class, except for the few who played together on the school rugby team. Pupils' attitudes to teachers were closely related to the stream to which they belonged, but even more closely related to this was their perception of what the teachers thought of them: 73 per cent of 4D boys thought that teachers had a negative opinion of them, as compared with only 10 per cent of 4A boys.

Teachers encouraged boys in the higher streams to think of themselves as different and superior, although it was often not until their third year that boys responded by behaving significantly 'better' than those in other streams. Misbehaviour in one of the top streams was commonly quelled by such remarks as 'You sound more like 1E than 3B', and some teachers actively discouraged A-stream pupils from mixing with those in other streams. The lower stream pupils were conscious of the lack of privileges they received, of the fact that teachers distrusted them and were not very interested in them or their future, and of the lack of demands for hard work placed upon them. Hargreaves found that the teachers given the task of teaching the lower stream classes adapted to this situation in one of two ways: some 'withdrew' from the situation, sitting at their desks doing paperwork or lecturing to the class in a loud voice, apparently not noticing that the pupils, engaged in other activities, were paying very little attention to them; others imposed a rigid discipline, obtaining a quiet classroom in which pupils were obliged to give the appearance of working, but were bored and uninvolved in their work and spent much of their energy in attempting to disrupt lessons without being detected.

Although we do not have much experience in Britain of non-streamed secondary schools, there can be little doubt that at all stages streaming exacerbates negative attitudes of both teachers and pupils and creates difficulties in teacher–pupil relations; and it is likely that, as most investigations have indicated, it has a detrimental effect upon the attainments of pupils in the lower streams. Yet the little available evidence indicates that the attitudes of teachers are of crucial importance; and the great majority of teachers are in favour of streaming. This suggests that most teachers are not well skilled in teaching classes with a wide range of pupil attainments, and that they realize this. That the abolition of streaming does not raise insoluble problems or detract severely from the attainments of the most able has been demonstrated in its successful implementation in such countries as the U.S.S.R., in that streaming is quite rare in Scottish primary schools, and by the experience of those few secondary schools in this country where streaming has been at least partially abolished. But a necessary condition for the success of non-streaming is that teachers should desire it and be confident of their ability to cope. One may question whether the skills of teaching children of varied abilities in one class are given sufficient attention at present, either in inservice or preservice training.

Team teaching. Conventionally, every teacher has the total responsibility for teaching a class of twenty to forty pupils one or more subjects for a term or more. One of the fundamental ideas of team teaching is that this stable class unit with its individual teacher is not always the form of social grouping which leads to most effective learning. A 'team' of several teachers, given the responsibility for the instruction of the pupils who would otherwise be in their separate classes, should be able, by using a variety of teaching techniques, and pupil groups of varied size and composition, to teach more effectively. Lectures, class teaching, group discussions, individual assignments and programmed instruction can all be incorporated in a programme in which teaching resources are allocated where they are thought to be most necessary. Team teaching projects have taken different forms and have had different goals, but among the benefits most commonly claimed have been:

1. Group size and composition can be modified to suit the task and the teaching method used.

2. Teachers may specialize in those aspects of subject content and in those teaching methods with which they are most experienced and able.

3. The services of non-professional staff, who become integral members of the team, may be more efficiently used, as can school equipment and rooms.

When working in a team, inter-teacher relations acquire a greater significance for each teacher. Much of the freedom that a teacher traditionally has in 'his own' classroom must be sacrificed. If teaching methods and the size and composition of pupil groups are to be varied appropriately, the team must be given more power to plan their own work than individual teachers usually have. But within the team, decisions have to be taken more explicitly and a greater amount of planning is required; at any one time, each teacher must have a clearly specified role, and if he does not do what his colleagues expect, he is likely to detract from the effectiveness of the group effort. The extra flexibility which the system allows in planning may thus be counteracted by a decrease in the flexibility with which each individual can approach his own teaching. Where the team includes ancillary and auxiliary staff, it is even more necessary to teach in accordance with a previously decided plan if their efforts are to be capitalized upon.

An important aspect of the work of a team is clearly the co-operative planning of their teaching. This requires new skills and knowledge, such as assessing each other's suitability for different roles and choosing the appropriate teaching method, from the wider range available, for each type of subject-matter. It also involves the skills of working as members of a committee. Research has revealed some of the features which commonly characterize successful committees. Among these are:

1. Different people adopt different roles, particularly those of the task leader, who keeps everyone's mind on the job, and of the social leader, who keeps the atmosphere harmonious; and, less often, of the 'ideas man', full of suggestions, and the 'strong silent man', who listens most of the time and weighs things up.

2. In terms of content, the general trend is through facts, then opinions, then suggestions, finally to decisions.

3. Members, especially those of high status, talk to the group rather than to other individuals; while they are talking, they look at the other members of the group, communicating non-verbally as well as verbally; similarly, other members constantly give active indications that they are listening.

Results such as these indicate that committee work involves skilled performances, and though teachers often work on committees in other contexts, in team teaching these skills become of more immediate importance.

Where teachers are working together, both in planning and in actual teaching, conflict between them becomes both more likely and more damaging in its consequences. If two members differ widely in their educational attitudes and goals, they are unlikely to be able to cooperate closely. Another potential source of conflict, which arises from the specialization of teaching roles within a team, is the allocation of a teacher to a role which does not satisfy the needs of his particular personality. For example, the person with a strong affiliative drive is unlikely to be satisfied with a predominantly lecturing role. A team has therefore to be chosen with attention being given to the attitudes and personalities of its members and their relation to the various roles required.

Team teaching projects have been so varied in nature

that it is impossible to generalize about the changes they may induce in teacher–pupil relationships. Certain forms of team teaching, however, have possible advantages. Where pupils are grouped for various purposes on different bases, as is more feasible when several teachers are working together, it is less likely that groups of pupils will be perceived in a stereotyped way either by their peers or by their teachers. Where some time is given to lectures and some to private study, and where pupils meet several teachers in the context of one 'class', they may acquire greater independence of teachers in their attitudes to learning, and may perceive 'the teacher' less as the unique authority figure of the conventional classroom. At the same time, contact with a teacher in small groups may allow less formal relationships with him to be developed. And where teachers adopt the roles of specialists to be consulted, pupils have the freedom to seek the advice of those teachers with whom they find relationships easiest.

The Classroom Group

Pupil norms and expectations for teacher behaviour

It might be expected that pupils, coming as they do from many different kinds of environment and to very different types of school, would vary widely in the teacher characteristics of which they most approve and disapprove. Yet the many investigations of pupils' likes and dislikes since the beginning of this century have produced results which show a high degree of unanimity. Evans (1962) summarizes the results of these studies thus:

Children like teachers who are kind, friendly, cheerful, patient, helpful, fair, have a sense of humour, show an understanding of children's problems, allow plenty of pupil activity and at the same time maintain order. They dislike teachers who use sarcasm and ridicule, are domineering and have favourites, who punish to secure discipline, fail to provide for the needs of individual pupils and have disagreeable personality peculiarities.

Whether these qualities are more liked or disliked in teachers than in other adults one cannot tell; but in one American investigation, comparing the teacher qualities liked or disliked by children and, retrospectively, by adults, it was found that children tended to be more concerned with the qualities of teachers as teachers, while adults judged them more in terms of personal attributes. A similar difference was found by Taylor (1962) between pupils and teachers: children, especially younger children, described 'the good teacher' more in terms of his teaching than did teachers or student-teachers; the latter group in particular emphasized the personal qualities of teachers. Taylor found wide agreement among pupils about the importance of firmness, justice, the avoidance of corporal punishment, friendliness, knowledge and, most of all, participation in class activities. Amongst junior school pupils, encouragement to work hard was stressed, as was politeness by the girls; and amongst secondary school pupils, cheerfulness and explaining the work were emphasized.

Rather less investigation has been made of how pupils *expect* teachers to behave, or of the consequences of such expectations for teacher–pupil relations. Expectations may be influenced by the extent and nature of a pupil's experience of teachers, stereotypes of teacher behaviour held by parents and other associates, or the stereotypes implicit in comics and television programmes. The more varied the behaviour of those teachers whom a pupil has previously encountered, the less definite will his expectations be. It is useful here to think in terms of the nomothetic (role-centred) and ideographic (person-centred) dimensions which Getzels applies to behaviour in social organizations. Teachers who stress the importance of children 'knowing how to behave in classrooms' attach importance to the nomothetic dimension and to the clear definition of the complementary roles of pupil and teacher. For such teachers, there are rules of behaviour to which pupils should learn to conform, and if these rules are different for different teachers, pupils are likely to become confused. In these circumstances, it is desirable that pupils should have clear expectations of teacher behaviour, and therefore that there should be a high degree of consistency in the behaviour of the various teachers in a school. Some teachers stress rather the ideographic aspect of classroom activity, accepting variations in pupils' behaviour according to their personal needs and themselves attempting to adapt their behaviour to help meet these needs. For these teachers, roles are much less clearly defined, and pupils are less likely to acquire, or to require, clear expectations of teacher behaviour. The greatest problems for pupils arise when, accustomed to teachers who stress appropriate role-behaviour, they encounter one who emphasizes personal needs, or vice versa. In the former case, they may miss the security of having to conform to clearly stated rules, and may, for example, consider the teacher to be unfair when he reacts differently to the same 'transgression' committed by different pupils. In the latter, they must learn that many situations are now rule-bound where they were not before and accustom themselves to a more formal relationship with the teacher. Either way, the teacher's behaviour is likely to be initially severely misunderstood because of the pupils' expectations.

One expectation of teachers which appears to be shared by many British pupils is that among their primary functions are those of policeman and judge in the classroom. While it is assumed that every teacher will attempt to carry out these functions, what is not known about a new teacher is how efficient a policeman he will be, or how severe a judge. And since these aspects of the teacher's role can only achieve primacy when much of the class's uncurbed behaviour is considered to be unlawful, the question commonly asked about a new teacher is 'How far, in our lawless behaviour, can we go with him?' A teacher entering this sort of situation who behaves as though these were not important functions, but as if his task were simply to instruct or as if he will be accepted as a friend, counsellor and stimulator of ideas, is not likely to be perceived as he perceives himself. He will rather be categorized by pupils as 'soft' and incompetent, and be given little respect.

The social structure of the classroom group

Among the pupils in every classroom, there are more or less stable patterns of interaction. The class may or may not be divided into several sub-groups; if there are such sub-groups, they may be hostile, friendly or tolerant towards one another; each member of the class may communicate with most others, only with those in his own sub-group, predominantly with one or two high-status members of the class, or very rarely with anyone. The nature of the class structure has important bearings on the type of relationships which it is possible for a teacher to establish with his pupils, and on the problems with which he is likely to be faced.

A class may be structured in two ways: a formal, organizational structure imposed by the teacher and an informal structure of friendship ties among pupils. The two may be quite independent of each other, although where the same formal organization is retained over a period of time, factors such as contiguity and shared status are likely to influence friendship patterns. Conversely, a teacher may take account of the informal group structure in organizing the class's work.

The formal social organization of a class includes such steps as the appointing of class monitors or otherwise prescribing specific roles for individuals, but usually the most fundamental aspect is the division of a class into several groups for teaching purposes. There are many bases upon which such groupings can be made, including common interests in particular projects, friendship groups, age (in small rural schools), or such criteria as house membership which give virtually random groups. The most popular basis, however, is assessed ability, either a general ability grouping used for most purposes, or grouping according to ability in specific subjects, such as reading and arithmetic. Research has not so far produced any clear conclusions as to whether such ability grouping has a desirable effect upon pupils' attainments, but something may be said about its social effects.

While flexibility of group composition is generally agreed to be desirable, it is often difficult to move a child up from one group to another without omitting a necessary step in learning the skill or knowledge involved. It is therefore normal for a child who starts in a low-ability group to remain in it, though a child in a higher group can easily be 'demoted'. An investigation by Kelley (1951) indicated the likely social consequences of such a situation. He divided a group into two sub-groups, in one of which the members were given a high status but were told that they might lose this at any time; the second sub-group was given a low status and made to believe that it could do nothing to achieve a higher status. For both sub-groups, membership of the group decreased in attractiveness and expressions of hostility between the two sub-groups grew. On the other hand, when a second group was divided so that those with high status believed they were secure in that position, and those with low status were told they could improve their position, the opposite occurred. It would seem that, if classes are to be grouped according to ability (and therefore into groups of different status, if pupils accept the teacher's values) the cohesiveness of the class and its attractiveness will decrease unless it is clearly possible to move from less to more able groups, and less likely that the reverse will occur.

The advantages gained from ability grouping in being able to grade the tasks given to pupils must be weighed against the social problems created. As with any form of grouping, the teacher needs to be more skilled and to make greater efforts in planning and in class management: he must be able to work with one group in the confidence that the others have tasks which they understand and which they are sufficiently motivated to complete without his assistance. But furthermore, many of the undesirable social effects of streaming are likely to occur within the classroom. Pupils, having been given an ascribed status, are likely to assess themselves and others in terms of this status and, as research has indicated, to overestimate their performance and their potential if they are of high status, and to underestimate these if they are of low status. In particular, pupils in the low ability groups are therefore likely to be over-conscious of their poor attainments and, where attainment is valued by most of the class, to be socially rejected by other pupils. A common reaction is to be hostile towards the abler pupils, towards the teacher, and towards school learning. The teacher may therefore face the triple problem of having several pupils who reject his values and efforts (which may occur without ability grouping), of having himself created conditions in which these uncooperative pupils tend to form a closely-knit minority group and thus to reinforce one another's rejection of him, and of having a class which is divided into hostile factions.

Whether or not a class has any formal social organization, it has an informal social structure which, with pupils over the age of about seven, and when the class has been together for some time, tends to be relatively stable. Subgroups of various sizes are formed, either integrated within a cohesive class group, or indifferent or hostile to other sub-groups. Within each group, members differ in status, that is in the prestige they hold and the influence which they have over other members, and also in popularity. Popularity and status, although often closely linked, are distinguishable: a bully may have high status but few friends. There are also usually differences in status among sub-groups. Membership of such informal groups is voluntary, and that members continue to belong to them is due to a shared acceptance of, and preference for, certain ways of behaving. Although extensive deviation from group norms will lead to a person being rejected by the group, those with highest status within a group have most freedom to deviate without fear of rejection. At the other extreme, individuals on the fringe of a group who desire acceptance are often the most conforming to prove their 'eligibility'.

One technique for discovering group structure is that of sociometry, whereby each individual is asked to name those with whom he would most like to engage in a given activity. It is then possible to draw up a 'sociogram', showing any sub-groups which exist, the relative popularity of each individual, and the general cohesiveness of the class. With such stable groups as school classes, the choices are usually very similar for most purposes, and it is often simpler and equally revealing to ask pupils whom they would prefer as friends; or, for some purposes, who their friends are. The examples shown in Figure 7 (adapted from Hargreaves, 1967) are of this last type; in this case pupils were asked to name their friends in the year-group, but only choices within each class are indicated. Sociometry is by itself a limited technique, which cannot reveal such things as the relative status of different sub-groups, the causes of their formation, or their norms. It is therefore best used together with other techniques, and Hargreaves supplemented the information revealed in the sociograms with observations, interviews and other questionnaires. Thus in Form 4A, group A is the sub-group of highest status, its members above average in academic achievement and greatly liked by teachers; its norms are of academic achievement, conscientiousness, regular attendance and punctuality, smartness of dress, cleanliness, no copying, no 'messing' in classes, no swearing and no fighting. Group C on the other hand is a low-status group, four of whose members had been in the B stream the previous year, relatively low in attainment, antagonistic to group A and not fully accepting its norms. Adrian in group A, the school captain, is the most liked boy in the class, and Alf in group C the most disliked; they dislike each other intensely.

Form 4C is more sharply divided into three sub-groups.

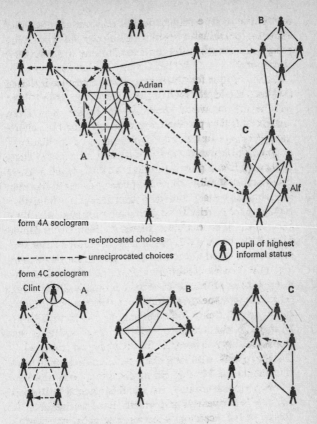

form 4A sociogram

——————————— reciprocated choices

- - - - - - - ▶ unreciprocated choices

pupil of highest
informal status

form 4C sociogram

*Figure 7. Sociograms for two secondary school classes
(Hargreaves, 1967)*

Group A, of highest status, is low in academic achievement and its norms are opposed to such attainment and to
work in class. Truancy and lateness are expected of its
members and copying, 'messing', hostile behaviour towards teachers and dressing so as to transgress school
rules are normative. Together with a group from 4D, it
forms a group for whose activities outside school bullying,

petty theft and other delinquent behaviour are normative. The boy with highest status in the class, Clint, is recognized as the best fighter in the school and uses this recognition in and out of class. Group C, whose members are well above class average in academic attainment, is of lowest status in the class.

These two classes exemplify several of the features which one may look for in any classroom. Neither class is very cohesive, though in both the values of one dominant clique are accepted by the majority of pupils. These values are in one case consistent with those of the teachers, in the other they are directly opposed. In each class there are two or three friends who are particularly influential, though in one case two of them are not very popular, and in both classes there are pupils who are isolated, not chosen by anyone. In both, the A and C groups are mutually hostile, the A and B groups mutually tolerant. Each of these features affects the teacher's task, on the one hand raising problems of social learning and adjustment which he may or may not attempt to deal with, and on the other determining the conditions in which he must attempt to communicate with the class and to arouse pupils' motivation to achieve the goals he sets them.

The cohesiveness of a class – the co-ordination of its members' efforts, the effectiveness of communication throughout the group, and its resistance to disruptive forces – is particularly important for the teacher. For one thing, the less energy is spent on internal dissension, the more time and energy is available for work. Also, with a cohesive class, the teacher's task is greatly simplified, since he can approach it (and the pupils him) as one body rather than as three or four groups or thirty or forty individuals. The teacher's own behaviour can affect the cohesiveness of a class. Form 4A at Lumley had been more cohesive the previous year, when its form-master stressed its exclusiveness and status, and encouraged pride in its corporate achievements. The more talking a teacher allows among pupils, and encourages by his teaching methods, the greater the mutual liking there tends to be among them and the greater the class cohesiveness (Bovard, 1956). Also relevant is the motivational technique used by teachers: experiments comparing the effects of competition between individuals or between groups with those of co-operative working have shown that communication is greater and more widespread, pupils are more friendly towards one another, there is more orderliness, and generally greater cohesiveness when the co-operative approach is used (e.g. Deutsch, 1960). Cohesiveness can also be increased when the teacher's behaviour is perceived as threatening to the class and its values. When this occurs, open hostility towards the teacher tends to be less restrained, the group's solidarity giving courage to its individual members. In such circumstances, the teacher may wish to reduce the cohesiveness of the class; one way of doing this is to be so threatening and punitive that fear reduces the interaction among pupils.

Another way in which teachers can influence the social structure of their classes is in their behaviour towards socially isolated pupils. When a child differs from the rest of the class in such respects as colour, accent, dress or behaviour patterns, pupils are often ready to follow a teacher's lead in mocking, disregarding or accepting the 'unusual' child; and while few teachers would deliberately encourage the social rejection of a pupil by his peers, children tend to be acutely perceptive of teachers' attitudes to them and their classmates. Depending on group norms, teachers can also encourage a class to reject individuals by being too attentive to them and giving them more praise than others, or by emphasizing their low achievements or nonconformist behaviour. It is often possible to help an isolate to become accepted by arranging for him to work in a group, the other members of whom are of high status, on a task to which he can make a valuable contribution. Such behaviour on the part of the teacher can modify a social structure which would otherwise be stable: Taylor (1952) found that the sociometric status of pupils was less stable in classes where 'progressive' teaching methods were used than in more 'traditional' classrooms, and suggested that this was because progressive teachers gave greater help to their pupils in the solution of their social problems. Attempts to make radical changes in the social structure of a class are not, however, generally successful; and Polansky (1954) found that teachers who accepted and supported the existing status structure tended to have better relations with their pupils than those who did not.

To support a status structure one must know what it is, and research (e.g. Bogen, 1954) confirms that teachers who are so informed do tend to have better relations with their pupils. Yet for many British teachers the social relationships among their pupils are of only minor interest and, perhaps because of this, wide variations have been reported in teachers' knowledge about the social structures in their classes, some showing a high degree of ignorance (e.g. Blyth, 1958). Another reason for this ignorance is that there are systematic tendencies for the personality characteristics of pupils which are most easily perceived, and those which are most valued, by teachers to differ from those most observed and valued by other pupils.

Overview

Most teachers spend most of their working time in classrooms alone with their pupils, and it is what happens during this time which very largely determines what effects they have on their pupils' learning. In one sense, the classroom group is very isolated: teacher and pupils must generally get on as best they can with a minimum of interference or help from anyone else. Neither teacher nor pupils can opt out of the situation simply because they may find it boring, fruitless or stressful; and for a teacher to ask for the presence of a colleague or even temporarily to expel a pupil from the room is often considered to be an indication of failure. It may be that this isolation of the teacher's position as sole authority in the classroom is an important factor in determining the behaviour of many teachers; though whether this is the case will not be known until more evidence is available about the behaviour of teachers in other circumstances, such as team teaching and open-plan schools.

In another sense, however, the classroom is far from isolated from a wider social context. It is almost a cliché of modern educational thinking that pupils' behaviour in the classroom derives very largely from their lives outside it. This wider environment affects their physical health, their emotional maturity, their intellectual development, their aspirations and their values; and it influences the expectations and norms which they hold for their own and their teachers' behaviour in school, and, of great importance in the classroom, their relationships with one another. But, as the evidence presented in this chapter has made clear, factors in this wider social environment also have a direct influence upon the attitudes, expectations and classroom behaviour of teachers.

The relative influence on teachers of the diverse factors which have been considered cannot yet be determined, since most investigations up to this time have been exploratory and have dealt with only a limited range of variables. It seems probable, however, that it is the characteristics of the institutions in which teachers work, rather than those of particular individuals, which are most likely to affect their behaviour. The role of the teacher certainly appears to be influenced by at least three categories of such institutional characteristics: first, the social position of the school – its traditional educational goals and social assumptions, and the social background of the majority of its pupils; second, the organizational structure of the school – the nature of the leadership offered by the headmaster, for example, and the channels of communication open among the staff and between them and others, such as parents, outside the school; and third, the way or ways in which pupils are grouped for teaching purposes. It is to variables within these three categories that future research might most profitably relate the behaviour of teachers towards their pupils.

4 Motivation in the Classroom

Teachers make more or less organized and successful attempts to foster the achievements of pupils and to regulate the general behaviour of their classes. They do so through the content of their teaching, through the sanctions they use, and through their personal relationships with pupils. In going from one classroom to another it is apparent that teachers differ greatly in the ways in which they seek to motivate pupils, and also, that pupils differ among themselves in the value they place upon education, in their aspirations, and in the responses they make to particular teachers and methods of teaching. What, then, are the motives which shape pupils' responses, what are the differences between teachers in their handling of these motives, and can we identify the teachers who are more skilful in this respect?

Three related aspects of motivation are specially relevant here: the sources, the techniques for encouraging appropriate responses from pupils, and the prior experiences of pupils. There are considerable disagreements over the classification of motives, needs and drives. However, it is useful to consider, on the one hand, socially acquired needs for affiliation, dominance and achievement, and, on the other, exploratory and curiosity drives which are assumed to be intrinsic to children. Both groups have a clear relevance to teaching. Intrinsic motives, for instance, are the basis of major educational theories concerning 'activity' and 'discovery' methods of teaching. However, for the practising teacher the second aspect, that of motivational techniques, probably holds the greatest interest. The concern about techniques is apparent in the perennial controversy over punishments, in the problems voiced by young teachers about the handling of classes, and in some of the criticism directed at professional training. Rather less attention is given to the third aspect, despite the fact that the motivational histories of pupils are essential matters in any discussions on sources and techniques of motivation in the classroom.

Social Motivation

Although the motivation of learning and of cooperative behaviour is often seen in terms of the rewards and punishments that are continually being applied in the classroom, these extrinsic sanctions must be regarded as an inadequate basis for explaining the behaviour of pupils. If teachers had to rely solely upon these techniques there would be little learning or cooperation. Rather, we should begin by looking to those sources of motivation arising intrinsically from the pupil in his encounters with the social and physical environments, and to those motives fostered through relationships with adults and other children.

Affiliation and dominance

Children and adults seek the company and attention of others, establishing varied and subtle patterns of intimacy, dependence and influence which in turn shape their perceptions of others and of themselves, and much of their subsequent behaviour. Motivation underlying much social and professional interaction can be described in terms of two major drives for (a) affiliation, characterized by the search for close, warm personal relationships, and for physical and perceptual contact; and (b) dominance, shown in efforts to control the thoughts, values and actions of others, and in attempts to gain recognition, admiration, and prestige.

The strength and manner of expression of these drives are shaped by childhood experiences with adults and peers. Two stages are recognizable: the formation of social and emotional attachments in early infancy and, later, the acquisition of personal values and modes of behaviour through relations with adults and the company of other children. Processes of identification, introjection and modelling are advanced by psychologists concerned with explaining and describing the second stage. The initial attachments depend upon the development in the child of perceptual recognition of others, the satisfaction of psychological needs, and physical contact. They are facilitated by neural development in the first year of life and by smiling and eye-following mechanisms. Studies of infant animals deprived of mothering and of peer contact (Harlow and Harlow, 1962), and of human infants raised in institutions where caretaking is scanty and inconsistent, and where they receive little stimulation (e.g. Goldfarb, 1955), indicate that both temporary intellectual lag and extended social maladjustment can occur, the latter in the form of inability to establish usual affiliative and dominance styles. At the second stage, parental models in particular provide widely different opportunities for learning and exercising affiliation, dominance and dependence, both in relation to the models themselves and towards peers and adults. As a consequence, particular patterns of rearing and exposure shape distinctive behaviours in the school-child, and the teacher finds himself faced with strongly ingrained traits, beliefs and values, and widely divergent kinds of responsiveness to himself, his techniques and the content of education.

Schools and other educational institutions give extensive opportunities for the expression of affiliation and dominance, and relations with other pupils and with teachers form a basis for the regulation of the individual's behaviour. Contact with other pupils, through the physical proximity existing in the classroom and school, leads to the formation of peer groups and to involved patterns of social interaction in which children become influential over or dependent upon others. Peer groups are important both for the pupil and the teacher. In the first place, since they offer pupils the means to satisfy particular needs to affiliate or influence, and since they provide extensive opportunities for satisfying powerful tendencies to evaluate our personal interpretations of the environment and of ourselves against the interpretations and perceptions of others, they act as means to simplify and confirm decisions as to legitimate values and behaviours to adopt.

Experimental studies by Asch (e.g. 1951) and others have demonstrated the operation of pressures towards agreement with majority judgements. The subject has been placed among confederates of the experimenter who have made a deliberately distorted judgement of a physical stimulus. Under these conditions it is common to find the subject moving toward the group judgement despite the contrary evidence to his senses. Studies of obedience, reported by Milgram (e.g. 1964), also demonstrate our readiness to carry out the wishes of others. The basic design here was to get adult subjects to administer varying levels of electric shock which they believed were being experienced by a 'victim' in another room. In this situation, despite the extreme levels of nervous tension shown by the subjects, twenty-six out of forty were prepared to obey the experimenter to the extent of giving shocks of over four hundred volts, and all were prepared to go up to three hundred. Furthermore, in situations where the subject performed in the midst of two confederates of the experimenter who called for increasingly powerful shocks to the victim, mean shock levels rose in response to the confederates' pressure.

These studies of obedience and group conformity not only have implications for the behaviour of individuals within groups, but also for teachers. To take two illustrations: where the peer group has values markedly contradictory to those of the teacher, then following the group may be frequently preferred by individual pupils despite the likelihood of conflict with the teacher and the risk of punishment; also, where teachers have good relations with their classes, individual pupils can be influenced by teachers taking advantage of the affiliative and social comparison needs within the peer group.

Group structures and processes not only help or hinder pupils' or teachers' attempts to establish standards of behaviour, but also affect pupils' responses to instruction. One question that arises here is whether teaching procedures which employ pupil-with-pupil co-operation lead to different results from those achieved in more traditional situations where pupils work in comparative isolation although they have common tasks. A study by Deutsch (1960), using students, was concerned with this, two groups being matched on ability then treated differently so that one solved tasks in a highly competitive setting while the other was arranged in small co-operating groups. In the co-operative situation there was more work output per unit time, more pressure to achieve, more friendliness and a more favourable evaluation of the situation and its effects on individuals. Work on children by Richardson (1948) and Hallworth (1952) in which they compared group versus class teaching is in agreement concerning pupils' preferences for the group arrangement, the better morale and the greater liking for the subject being studied, but neither clearly demonstrated any superiority in learning in the groups. Also, Richardson pointed out that if groups are to be advantageous in terms of liking and morale then the members must want to work together, the group size has to be carefully adjusted to the task, and the groups should contain someone who can lead without being too dominant.

Such a variety of factors can be built into experimental or classroom groups that it is quite unrealistic to expect neat generalizations about the superiority of grouping over other arrangements, or about the advantages of some particular form of grouping. What we can see are some of the potential advantages of groupings, the problems facing the teacher in creating the situation that suits him and his pupils, and the high degree of management skills desirable. In the classroom, groupings based upon educational objectives have to be reconciled with those which would arise if pupils were expressing their own preferences. Too much emphasis upon a task-centred arrangement can cut across preferred affiliations and produce groups in which strong antagonisms exist, or in which the absence of cohesive influence structures leads the groups into spending much of their time on amiable but aimless social activities. On the other hand, pupil preferences can lead to groups varying greatly in size, and with restricted ranges of abilities and interests. Secondly, what is achieved by grouping will depend upon how clear the teacher is about his objectives and upon his knowledge of peer group relations and pupils' skills. Thirdly, some teachers lack ability to manage grouping and create more problems than they solve. And, finally, the use of co-operative procedures cannot be based upon current fashions alone: account must be taken of pupils' prior experience, so that to place some pupils in a teacher-contrived situation and then to expect increased self-control and greater responsiveness to teaching is unreasonable when they may have had a long history of imposed competitiveness and rigid control. These are not arguments to be used to dismiss grouping and co-operation, but rather indications of the kind of careful thinking that needs to be undertaken both by the individual teacher and the school.

Achievement motivation

Pupils manifestly differ in their responses to instruction; some strive to do well, others idle along or flag, some get down to the tasks in hand whether they like them or not, whilst others require the vigilance and support of the teacher. These differences may ultimately be reflected in the length of school careers, some staying on to advanced courses, whilst others take the first opportunity to throw off the burden of school.

Explanations proffered for these differences in response have included such school factors as 'poor' teaching, streaming and selection procedures, and influences stemming from the home and neighbourhood upon attitudes towards education.

Some social psychologists have given particular attention to rearing practices, viewing response to school as a function of acquired need for achievement – an impetus to do well relative to some standard of excellence. Study of achievement motivation stemmed from McClelland's work (e.g. McClelland *et al.*, 1953) on the causes of technological and economic change, in which he argued that the motivations of the dominant members in a society play a major role in change, in particular the motivation in such persons to work primarily for the sense of having done their job well. This work has subsequently led to investigations of early influences which might account for differences in achievement motivation between individuals and between groups. This motive has typically been assessed by the use of projective techniques in which subjects have been asked to write stories in response to scenes portrayed on cards. Children, for example, may be shown a card of a boy looking at a desk in a room, then asked to say what they think is happening, what happened before, and what will happen. Individuals scoring high on achievement motivation as assessed by these means have commonly been reported as showing greater preference for moderately difficult tasks, preference for moderate risks in tasks involving skill and ability, greater self confidence, and more readiness to put off immediate reward for later gratification.

Evans (1967), reporting on the effects of achievement motivation and ability upon discovery learning – the task being to find the principles of encoding, and then to decode factual statements, in a number of cryptograms – found that students high in achievement motivation spent more time on the learning task and were superior in it.

With children, achievement motivation has been shown at one time or another to correlate positively with social class, assignment to school stream, age, and intelligence, but where these factors have been studied in relationship to one another (Bruckman, 1966) intelligence has remained as the single persisting association – although the correlation, typically about + 0·3, indicates that achievement motivation is not so closely dependent on intelligence that it cannot be regarded as a significant variable in its own right.

No neat explanation in terms of supposed differences in social class rearing practices is tenable. Children who score high on the tests are likely to come from families where the mothers lay stress on independent mastery – leading other children, self-assertion, making one's own friends and attempting difficult tasks without help – and where parents typically set high standards for the child's work, coupled with expression of warmth and emotional involvement for good work. Low motivation appears to be associated with parents who make strong demands for routine compliance, who are indulgent and willing to accept low standards of work.

However, achievement need as conventionally assessed has not proved a good predictor of scholastic achievement, one possible reason being that we are dealing here with a general behaviour trait that is not necessarily manifested in response to school. Academic motivation may be a more specific aspect, and Entwhistle (1968) has been working on the development of a self-rating inventory for its assessment, containing items on attitudes to school, aspirations, work habits and determination to do well. This has already been shown to discriminate between pupils who improved or deteriorated on academic performance after their transfer to secondary schools.

From another but related angle, educational studies of home and school factors in school achievement also bring out the importance of parental attitudes to school and education. Wiseman (1964) in a study of secondary school children has identified a factor of maternal psychological care which is associated particularly with reading performance, and Peaker summarizes findings presented in the Plowden Report (Children and their Primary Schools,

1967) by saying that, 'more of the variation in children's school achievement is specifically accounted for by variations in parental attitudes than either by variations in material circumstances of parents or by variations in schools.'

Bearing in mind that the expression of high achievement motivation in test scores does not necessarily mean that a pupil will work hard, will be academically successful or will be endowed with a special capacity to learn from his mistakes, nevertheless, indications of such motivation provide teachers with a further source of instructional effectiveness and control. The present relative emphasis of the effect of parental practices and attitudes does not mean that the contribution of the teacher is unimportant, but rather that he in fact may be able to do much more to reduce the effects of parental variations and increase the relative contribution of school among the factors influencing educational responses. In the first place, either directly through contacts with parents, or indirectly, but perhaps more potently, through the kinds of experiences of school to which teachers expose the adolescents who will soon become parents themselves, attitudes and behaviours can be fostered which will in their turn stimulate rather than discourage aptitude and enthusiasm. Secondly, specific aspects of teacher behaviour in the classroom may be influential: the extent to which teachers of the youngest pupils help them to understand the purposes and expectations of school; the avoidance of rigid practices of classifying pupils, which can depress the expectations of teachers and pupils, leading to a downward spiral of low aspirations and poor educational performance; and the setting of high standards by the teacher himself so that he provides an appropriate model for his pupils.

Intrinsic motivation

Here we shall begin by considering what happens when a young child is placed in an environment containing a number of unfamiliar objects. Initially he will make tentative approaches to the objects, then these inspections will be followed first by attempts to manipulate the objects, as if to determine their possibilities, and secondly by their active incorporation into a series of play behaviours. Finally, when the apparent possibilities have been exhausted, the child will leave the objects and move on to other activities. This is a common enough observation and would hardly attract more than amused attention if it were not that the child appears to be highly motivated. But how? There is no evidence of the application of conventional rewards or punishments, no adult presence is required to instigate or direct the activity, nor is the child motivated by discomfiting physiological states as hunger or thirst.

Human beings and other animals actively seek sensory stimulation and the opportunity to explore and manipulate the unfamiliar in situations where no extrinsic reward is provided and even where aversive stimuli are applied. Students paid to undergo sensory deprivation experiments, during which they were made physically comfortable but prevented from getting much of the usual sensory input from the environment, generally asked after two or three days to have the experiment ended, made repeated demands during the period for the most trivial of outside stimulation, and reported increased confusion, lack of concentration, irritability and hallucinations. Nursery school children, put in situations where the proportions of novel to familiar toys were varied, showed preferences for situations of intermediate novelty. Finally, studies of animals have shown, for example, that monkeys will work for long periods on simple wire puzzles without any extrinsic reward, and that rats will choose routes in mazes which lead to areas containing relatively more varied objects than other areas, even where such routes involve punishment by electric shocks.

These and many other findings point to a fundamental source of motivation, intrinsic to children and others, to search and to interpret their social and physical environments. It is from this continuous interaction between the child and his world that we can explain the growth of intelligence, the formation of social and emotional attachments and the acquisition of social values.[1]

Writing on the motivation of pupils, Hebb (1955) cites an experiment in a Canadian high school in which the pupils were told that they need do no work unless they wanted to, and that punishment for misdemeanours was to be sent out from the classroom, while the reward for being good was to be allowed to do more work. In these circumstances all the pupils soon discovered that within limits they preferred work, and learned more arithmetic than they had in the previous year. Many teachers might hesitate to make such radical demands upon a source of motivation that seems alien to many pupils. Nevertheless, liking for work, and the inherent control that goes with it, is commonplace among children. Yet teachers often report lack of interest and take recourse to extrinsic sanctions. Children start school with enthusiasm but for some it is soon lost. Why should this be? Perhaps this early response is simply due to the passing novelty of school for pupils who have neither the values appropriate to education nor sufficient capacity to find sustained satisfaction in mental activity? Perhaps motivation through curiosity and novelty is stronger at some stages of development than others, needing to be increasingly supplemented by extrinsic sanctions and by the other socially acquired motives? Thus, it is sometimes argued that while 'discovery' techniques are effective with younger pupils, the older ones 'need' to be taught. However, although some children may show only a brief reaction to the novelty of school and appear to require a great deal of deliberate

1. These notions about motivation are extensively represented in Piaget's developmental psychology (Flavell, 1963), in the work of Hebb (1955) and of Miller *et al.*, (1960), on the organization of behaviour, and in several cognitive theories of attitude change, for example, that of Festinger (1957) on cognitive dissonance.

effort to keep them active in their work, all children continue to manifest their enthusiasm for exploration and persistent effort in many other areas of activity – intrinsic motivation has hardly disappeared because response to school is poor. And while other forms of motivation, influenced by parents, peers and the larger community, certainly grow in relative importance it cannot be supposed that they eliminate earlier motives.

Perhaps, then, we should be looking at the skills of teachers in organizing their instruction and in providing compensatory conditions for poorly motivated pupils? Which aspects of teaching are most worth looking at in this context? It may be that some teachers have not acquired the techniques needed to take advantage of intrinsic motives in situations where they have to stimulate response to specific educational material. Indeed, there may be situations in which intelligent curiosity is stifled in all but the most determined pupils. There is little doubt that even at the most superficial level it is much more difficult to manage a class of individuals pursuing carefully guided and graded activities at different speeds and levels of achievement – that is, to provide the circumstances in which motivation comes from the interaction between the individual and the task rather than from imposed requirements of the teacher. Young teachers sometimes find themselves in the difficult position of having notions on organizing lessons around 'discovery' and 'activity' without having either the management skills or the extensive knowledge of pupils and appropriate tasks necessary to put the notions into effective practice. In these circumstances it is easy to fault the pupils rather than themselves, and to fall back on other instructional procedures. Changing the emphasis of motivation in the classroom is difficult and it will hardly work if the teacher is just going through the motions, for it not only requires management abilities of a high order, but also a radical change in the relationships he has with pupils.

Classroom Styles and Techniques

Styles and responses

Numerous attempts have been made to categorize teachers in terms of the general motivational styles they adopt. These categorizations often bear a close relation to the distinction between practices which emphasize learning through discovery and self-directed activity, and learning in closely directed and extrinsically motivated conditions.

A well known comparison of general styles is that between so-called authoritarian and democratic teachers. This stemmed from the social psychology of Kurt Lewin and his followers (e.g. Lippitt and White, 1943), and although it was initially applied in studies of children's club groups under different styles of leaders, the possible relevance to educational arguments over teacher-centred and learner-centred classrooms soon made for a popular line of investigation. The descriptive distinction applied here has been between:

Authoritarian – teacher-centred classroom, with high teacher dominance, formal class teaching, convergent thinking, competitiveness, relatively high punitiveness, low pupil verbal and physical activity, and teacher directed communication.

Democratic – learner-centred, less teacher dominance, pupil participation in class decisions, stress on pupils' ideas and divergent thinking, greater concern for individual needs for instruction, high pupil verbal and physical activity, cooperation, group structuring and more open teacher-pupil and pupil-pupil communication.

Ryans (1960) in his study of the characteristics of teachers has taken a different approach. Instead of resting his discussion upon a rather ill-defined distinction, he has attempted to establish major patterns of teacher classroom behaviours through applying systematic observation and rating of the characteristics of a large number of teachers.

He has identified three general ways in which teachers differ in their behaviour:

Warm, understanding, friendly versus aloof, egocentric, restricted behaviour.

Responsible, businesslike, systematic versus evading, unplanned, slipshod behaviour.

Stimulating, imaginative versus dull, routine behaviour.

These variables do not individually represent particular types of teachers; rather, it is the patterns in which they are combined in individuals which characterize their teaching.

What evidence is there on teachers' styles and pupils' responses? Wiseman (1964) used ratings of the 'progressiveness' of schools (progressiveness is generally identified with learner-centred styles of teaching) as one of a larger number of home and school measures, and found that pupils' achievements in the basic skills of reading and arithmetic were superior in the more 'progressive' schools, the associations being more pronounced in secondary schools. Ryans himself found that 'productive' pupil behaviour in the elementary school was related to the friendly-systematic-stimulating pattern of teacher behaviour.

In recent years a great deal of interest has been shown in convergent and divergent modes of thinking in pupils and in the role of the teacher in fostering 'creative' thinking (e.g. Torrance, 1960; Wallach and Kogan, 1965; Hudson, 1967). In this context, it is often said that our schools stress the acquisition of routine skills and intensive information and neglect to foster originality and high grade skills in problem-solving. This criticism has led to efforts to identify characteristics of teachers and teaching which influence the development of divergent thinking abilities, and also, more specifically, which help highly able children to profit fully from their education. This latter group, it is further claimed, includes many children who find school frustrating and lacking in stimulation.

Some of the work here has been done at the level of rather gross distinctions between schools. For example, in a recent British study Haddon and Lytton (1968) compared the scores of pupils on open-ended tests of divergent thinking in 'formal' and 'informal' schools. The pupils in the 'informal' primary schools were significantly superior on these tests. In describing the characteristics of the schools the workers on the study emphasized that this was not a comparison between good and bad schools, but rather that the 'informal' schools were more successful in fostering performance on these kinds of tests. Also, in seeking to identify what were the most important features of the 'informal' schools, they claim that it was not the degree of permissiveness but rather the emphasis upon self-initiated learning, the freedom of access, often unsupervised, to school libraries, relatively less use of class teaching and the relaxed, friendly atmosphere.

Other studies have looked at more specific teaching programmes for improving the fluency, originality and flexibility of thinking of pupils. Torrance (1961), for example, trained young children in how to produce ideas and reported that these pupils produced performances on 'creativity' tests superior to those of untrained children. Crutchfield (1966) used programmed instruction to take children through a series of creative problems to a successful solution of each of the problems. He found that trained pupils were superior to control children on various aspects of effective problem-solving, aspects such as questioning, production of good ideas, intelligent use of cues, and, finally, hitting on ideas which gave solutions to problems.

It is difficult to make generalizations from the findings of either the earlier studies on teacher- or learner-centred teaching styles, or the more recent ones focused on the divergent and convergent thinking abilities of pupils. A review of thirty-two of the earlier studies (Anderson, 1959) showed that eleven reported superior learning in learner-centred classes, eight reported superior learning in teacher-centred classes, and thirteen found no differences.

A more recent review (Parnes and Brunelle, 1967) of forty studies reported that 'creative' production (fluency, originality and elaboration) was significantly increased by most of the deliberate educational programmes that were used.

Some of the inconsistencies between the findings of various studies can be attributed to differences in definitions of the teaching styles or methods under investigation, to the different kinds of assessments made, and to unjustified assumptions that teachers classified on the basis of tests or impressionistic ratings will manifest distinctive patterns of teaching or personal relationships in the classroom.

However, there is sufficient agreement among studies for three points to be made. Most pupils prefer classrooms where teachers use 'discovery' methods and where they establish relatively democratic relationships. Teacher-centred situations, in which there is a great deal of expository teaching, tend to produce more learning where the tasks are relatively straightforward and emphasize the acquisition of routine information and skills. Learner-centred teaching, where more attention is given to individual and group work, where pupils are encouraged under guidance to seek solutions to problems, and where they are stimulated to produce and develop their own ideas, often seems preferable where the tasks are more complex, and where insightful and cooperative behaviours are primary objectives.

A search for some generally superior form of teaching has limited value. In its place two lines of development are worth following. One is towards the clearer specification of the methods which are most appropriate for fostering this or that group of abilities. The second is towards a fuller understanding of the effects of the interaction of the particular needs and abilities of pupils and teachers upon the working relationships established in the classroom and upon the quality of thought and feeling shown by pupils.

Teacher and pupil personalities

The behaviours of teachers and pupils are more than the spontaneous and short-lived outcomes of a particular situation. Each individual in the classroom brings with him characteristic attributes of personality which influence both the manner in which he behaves towards others and the ways in which they respond to him. The teacher with pervasive authoritarian characteristics is likely to reflect them in his interpretations of the motives of others and in the techniques he uses in his relationships. The pupil who is perceived as cooperative and highly motivated will establish a different relationship with others from the one who is troublesome and lacking in persistence. Thus, beneath the neat generalizations we may try to make about a particular style of teaching, the qualities of individuals will interact in a diversity of ways important to their social and educational behaviour.

Past attempts to predict patterns of teachers' behaviour from their performance on personality tests were not noticeably successful. However, a promising line of inquiry has developed from Harvey *et al.*'s (1966) analysis of teachers' personalities in terms of abstractness–concreteness. Concreteness is defined as a disposition towards fixed and categorical beliefs, authority rather than task concern, and a preference for a simple-structure environment. In the classroom, teachers with these characteristics are more likely to impose goals, provide detailed means to attainment, and show less tolerance of pupils' deviations from goals and standards. They are more likely to make use of functional explanation of rules and of unexplained rules, are particularly concerned with laying down procedure, and are more punitive. Abstractness, characterized by flexible and sophisticated belief systems and preference for a complex-structure environment, is associated with greater warmth towards pupils, more perceptiveness of pupils' needs, flexibility in meeting needs and interests, relaxed classroom relationships, task involvement and child participation. These differences are reflected in pupils' responses. In a study of kindergarten and first grade children and their teachers (Harvey *et al.*, 1968), teachers were rated on classroom indications of resourcefulness, dictatorialness and punitiveness. Their pupils were rated on cooperation, involvement, activity, achievement and helpfulness. Pupils of the 'abstract' teachers were significantly more involved in classroom activities, more active and higher in achievement than their counterparts. Other studies have confirmed that concreteness of belief systems is associated in teachers with markedly greater use of punishment, with less awareness of the possible variety of ways in which diagnostic and remedial issues may be resolved, and with tendencies to making quick and inflexible judgements early in a sequence of information on pupils (e.g. Joyce, Lamb and Sibol, 1966).

Although a great deal of effort has gone into the classification of teacher characteristics, this has rarely been done for pupils – too often treated as a mere collection of responses without personalities of their own. However, the early work on children's club groups brought out the fact that individuals could respond in markedly different ways to a leader – the authoritarian leader, for example, could be preferred by a child even though this was not a general preference in the group. Unfortunately, little work has subsequently been done to get at the interactions between distinctive personalities. However, one study strongly suggests that it is well worth while doing so. Washburne and Heil (1960) classified teachers as 'spontaneous', 'orderly' and 'fearful', further sub-dividing them into those who were 'superior' or 'inferior' according to their warmth and responsiveness to pupils. Pupils were classified as 'strivers', 'docile conformers' and 'opposers'. All possible combinations of the teachers and pupils were then examined in relation to pupils' achievements. Leaving aside for the moment the pupil differences in personality, teachers ranged in effectiveness (as assessed against pupils' achievements) from the 'superior orderly' (warm, relatively dominant and businesslike) through to the 'superior spontaneous' (warm, exuberant, highly independent, with a strong liking for expression of ideas), and down to the 'superior fearful' (warm, dependent, severely conscientious, and fearful of a threatening environment). The least effective were the 'inferior spontaneous'. When pupil differences were taken into account, then strivers did well more or less regardless of the characteristics of the teacher; docile conformers did exceptionally well with superior spontaneous teachers; whilst opposers, who as a whole did relatively poorly for all teachers, were most responsive to the superior orderly.

In any class the personality differences or similarities of teachers and pupils can influence the educational responses of pupils. Present schools, organized about the unit of one teacher and his class, lead to random wholesale encounters which minimize the impact of particular teachers upon particular pupils. Thelen (1967) has argued persuasively about the need for individual matching of teacher and pupil for improving 'teachability', but to achieve this would entail radically different timetabling from that which now commonly operates, and schools designed for flexibility rather than as standard class units.

Sanctions in the classroom

This and the following section deal with teachers' views and practical techniques concerning school and classroom behaviour. In doing so it is useful to begin by asking what teachers themselves see as the most frequent and serious problems in their classrooms, and which techniques they use in dealing with them. The most comprehensive study of their views was done by Highfield and Pinsent (1952), based upon a survey of some seven hundred teachers in English primary and secondary schools. These teachers reported two groups of difficulties in connexion with pupils' behaviour, which concerned them in that they affected professional responsibility, personal integrity, and their conception of social and moral order. The first consisted of restlessness, indifference, apathy, laziness, boisterous noisy behaviour, persistent carelessness, deceit and quarrelling – difficulties related to poor attitudes to school work and lack of motivation. At issue here was the teacher's professional responsibility towards the class. The second group consisted of more serious offences against a code of approved behaviour: malicious destructiveness, wilful disobedience, bullying, stealing, lying, cheating and persistent truancy. Such offences were seen as largely restricted to a small minority of really troublesome pupils, estimated by the teachers as 9 per cent of primary, 7 per cent of secondary modern, and 3 per cent of grammar school children. Within types of schools they recorded that percentages increased as one moved from upper to lower ability groups.

Teachers' opinions on the uses of various techniques closely reflected the two groups of problems with pupils. The most frequently used rewards were verbal appreciation, good marks, and recognition through test results, whilst the forms of blame and punishment, in decreasing order of frequency of reported use, were urging to make an effort, reprimand, warning of impending punishment, deprivation of marks, isolation, detention, light corporal punishment, sending to a higher authority, and corporal punishment. The majority were opposed to the use of corporal punishment for the first group of problems, such as laziness, untidy work, repeated errors and apathy, but clearly felt that it should be used for the second group – but as a last resort when other techniques had failed. Some 89 per cent of the teachers favoured the retention of corporal punishment in some form and the more recent findings of the survey carried out by the Plowden Committee show that as far as primary schools are concerned the position has remained largely unchanged over the space of fifteen years.

What evidence is there on the effects of techniques employed by teachers? Highfield and Pinsent's results represent the views of practitioners and their pupils, and show that teachers considered the most effective rewards to be quiet appreciation, election to posts of responsibility, public praise, and good team and class marks. Corporal punishment, referral to higher authority, deprivation of privileges and reports to parents were regarded as the most effective sanctions. However, pupils themselves ranked in order of effectiveness, reports to parents, referral to higher authority, loss of privileges and corporal punishment, and, as incentives, reports to parents followed by success in tests and good marks. Clearly they were less impressed by corporal punishment and much more concerned about what parents thought.

In addition to such evidence, there is an extensive body of experimental findings on verbal praise and blame, and other techniques. Kennedy and Willcutt (1964), surveying the results of over thirty studies of scholastic performance, physical activity and motor-tasks learning, conclude that both praise and blame are superior to practice alone, and that praise generally acts as a facilitator whilst blame has a depressing effect upon performance. The available evidence is remarkably consistent in view of the many factors which must be involved in determining responses to praise and blame – variations in the personal histories of pupils, prior patterns of reinforcement, differences in age and ability, and teachers' characteristics. Of course, there are differences: extraverts respond better to blame and introverts to praise; and where a pupil has a close relationship with the teacher, punishment in the forms of withdrawal of teacher approval or physical punishment are more likely to have effects than where no such relationship exists. However, the results in general are a strong argument for dispensing with blame techniques.

Punitiveness ranges from the use of verbal blame, through threats of some form of deprivation or punishment to the actual use of corporal punishment. There is no doubt that verbal and physical punishment can act as a deterrent and decrease the frequency of a behaviour, but such effectiveness as it has must be balanced against the further problems it can create, and against the likelihood that it is the least effective among a number of possible courses of action.

Where punishment is frequently used by a teacher and with little discrimination, it has depressing effects on the aspirations and future performance of pupils; it has no remedial value whatsoever for pupils who have persisting and serious behaviour disturbances; and although it may have effect at the time of application this is shortlived. Furthermore, it is tiring to maintain as a method of control and can create unnecessary insecurity and hostility throughout the class. Punishment can aggravate difficulties with class control, for the behaviour of the teacher towards one pupil cannot be isolated from side effects upon others. This may be seen, for example, when a teacher with uncertain control has a confrontation with a particularly troublesome pupil. The intent to quell the trouble and strengthen the teacher's authority can degenerate into a display of threats and counter-threats which make the teacher ridiculous before the class, reinforcing the chance that the troublesome pupil and others will engineer further episodes for their amusement.

Even where punitiveness is apparently effective in getting docile conformity, which may create a gratifying impression of 'good discipline', it fails to develop a genuinely internal self-control among pupils, so that the troublesome behaviour continues in other situations. Sometimes young teachers not only suffer from their own limited skills but also from having to cope with unco-operative pupils whose behaviour has been essentially unaffected, or even aggravated, by experienced teachers who, superficially solving their own problems of discipline, fail entirely to get at the real issues. Moreover, teachers may serve as models on which pupils shape their behaviours. Since there is little work on the process of social modelling in the classroom it is difficult to say how important the influence of teachers is, but there is extensive evidence on parent and other adult models influencing both deviant and pro-social behaviours of children (Bandura and Walters, 1965; Bryan, 1968). A study by Kounin and Gump (1961) has, however, shown that punitive teachers may produce children who not only display more overt aggression than those of non-punitive teachers, but also greater conflicts over what is right and not right behaviour in school. Also, where counter dominance and aggression is shown by children, it may not be directed at the original model but rather at other adults and peers (Lippitt and White, 1943).

Although there is little doubt about the general superiority of praise techniques and about the disadvantages of more extreme forms of punishment, there remains the fact that teachers often have to get pupils to do things they have no wish to do and have to stop particular behaviours. In particular, a small proportion of pupils, varying very much in numbers from school to school, are very troublesome and disproportionately disruptive in the classroom as well as being a harm to themselves and their prospects. While most pupils will respond to the usual techniques, so that with them it is a matter of applying the general findings on rewards and punishments, the more troublesome can be singularly unresponsive, at least in the short term, and require special consideration.

Troublesome pupils

Pupils with behaviour disturbances fall into two broad categories: those with what are often called conduct problems, such as marked disobedience, destructiveness, restlessness, distractibility and impulsiveness; and those with so-called personality problems, revealed in feelings of inferiority, self-consciousness, aloofness, day-dreaming and lethargy. Although these are rather arbitrary categories the two behaviour patterns, which appear consistently in studies of children and adolescents, relate to different kinds of difficulties facing teachers; on the one hand, those concerning classroom control and the effective treatment of pupils who are disorderly and who disrupt the work and relationships of teachers and other pupils; and on the other, those having to do with helping the under-reactive and inhibited pupil to find more satisfaction in his personal relationships and schoolwork. Both kinds of pupils mean additional and skilful treatment in the classroom, but the very immediacy of conduct problems commonly means that they attract more attention, although not necessarily more effective teacher behaviour.

One approach to the control of really troublesome pupils is to treat the matter in terms of the general class management skills of teachers. A study by Kounin, Friesen and Norton (1966) looked at control from this aspect when they took normal classes containing emotionally disturbed children and watched and recorded the teachers at work. Those teachers who were successful with the non-disturbed pupils were also relatively successful with the disturbed, having less deviant behaviour and apparently producing a classroom climate which contained their misbehaviour and prevented it from disrupting that of others. While there was no indication that certain types of personality were more successful than others, certain aspects of management did appear to be influential; in particular, the teacher's ability to communicate to the class that she knew what was going on around her. Teachers who could convey the impression that they had 'eyes in the back of their heads' had more work involvement and less deviancy. Secondly, those who had the ability to make smooth transitions from one class activity to another were at an advantage. Too much activity change, coupled with the mishandling of changeovers, overloading of pupils with instructions about activities and the interruption of newly begun ones by references back to past work and performance, all helped to create unnecessary opportunities for bad behaviour. This study is obviously limited, nevertheless it does point clearly to quite specific points of management as the sources of a lot of trouble.

A further difficulty which teachers may give themselves lies in their creating over-permissive situations. Disapproval of the methods and outcomes of authoritarian techniques has sometimes led to the advocacy of permissiveness. There are undoubtedly some highly skilled teachers who can achieve considerable success by such approaches. However, most cannot, and the great danger here is to confuse the highly skilled use of permissiveness with a wishy-washy, *laissez faire* approach. As part of their experimental work on forms of leader control of club groups of ten year olds, Lippitt and White introduced such a condition, characterized by complete freedom for the group or individual decision, a minimum of leader participation, no attempts by the leader to appraise or regulate the course of events or to participate in the group's activities, and by no information being supplied by the leader unless asked. Although the size and recreational nature of these groups mean that no strict comparisons can be made with the classroom the findings are interesting. The desire of at least some boys to accomplish something was continually frustrated by lack of adult leadership. Consequently, a great deal of time was spent in aimless activity, or in relatively inefficient efforts to establish peer leadership as an alternative to adult intervention. In turn, these led to dissatisfaction and poor coordination of effort. Lippitt and White say: 'The adult restrictiveness of the benevolent authoritarian role and the environmental unstructuredness of the *laissez faire* situation were both found to inhibit greatly genuine "psychological freedom" as contrasted to "objective freedom".' If we wish to foster pupils' accomplishments and self-control then it must be done actively by the teacher and not by allowing them to do as they wish. This applies to all children, but perhaps particularly to the really troublesome who are most in need of help from others.

One answer to the problem of the troublesome pupil is

to be found in developing school policies which minimize the chances of deviant behaviour arising and flourishing rather than in attempts, often when matters have gone too far, to change effectively the pupil's behaviour. There is some evidence to show that schools play an important part in a community cycle of delinquency. As part of a study carried out in a London borough (Power *et al.*, 1967) data were obtained for a period of six years on the incidence of delinquency in relation to schools attended by pupils and to the neighbourhoods in which they lived. Among some twenty secondary modern schools, taking 85 per cent of all eleven to fourteen year old pupils in the borough, the incidence rate for court appearances of boys (where cases were proven) varied from 0·7 to 7·8 per 100, and the annual average of all cases proven by the courts from 0·9 to 19 per 100. Considering that the period covered allowed for a succession of pupils through the schools and not simply one intake, these results show systematic differences in the incidence of delinquency. Several explanations might be offered – the physical conditions of schools, ability and ethnic differences, pupil transfers tending to concentrate troublesome pupils in some schools, and variations in police practices across neighbourhoods – but none of these gave an adequate explanation. There was the further possibility that neighbourhood characteristics might account for the school differences, and this was examined by taking a number of schools and analysing delinquency in terms of incidence within each school for those pupils who came from high and low delinquency neighbourhoods. This, however, only partly accounted for school differences. It seems that some schools were clearly contributing a larger share than others. Unfortunately no attempt is made to explore how the schools differed in their policies.

Earlier work by Clegg (1962), carried out in a group of Yorkshire schools, examined delinquency against both neighbourhood background and the use of punitive methods in schools. He found a positive association between the use of corporal punishment in the schools and the incidence of delinquency. Again, since this might have been explained in terms of some schools being in poorer districts, data were obtained on neighbourhood housing and economic conditions, but there was little association between these variables and either delinquency or the extent of use of the cane. Whilst the results do not, of course, establish the direction of causation (if indeed simple direction is involved) between delinquency and school punishment, there is nothing in these findings to invalidate the view that corporal punishment aggravates troublesome behaviour, and nothing to support the common argument that it is necessary in poorer school neighbourhoods in order to maintain discipline. Commenting upon the results Wiseman (1964) says, 'This suggests that far from caning reducing delinquency, it may well be increasing it . . . the use of corporal punishment leading to the early establishment of the "us" and "them" attitude, and the development of hostility to authority of all forms.'

The teacher's awareness of the many sources, and of the early signs of troublesome behaviour can be important in deciding upon an effective policy. For example, one argument about pupils who are persistently troublesome is that the great majority are 'normal' children or adolescents in the context of an unsatisfactory background. However, Stott (1966) has maintained that an important minority of such pupils manifest a wide range of symptoms of maladjustment, indications of multiple impairment – behaviour disturbance, physical defect, proneness to infections and early hospitalization – and vulnerability to stressful situations. If this argument is accepted then it points in the first place to the possibility of predicting children who are likely to become seriously troublesome (in school, and of course in other contexts) and of tackling the problem at its early stages. He has devised a preliminary screening instrument of six questions which might be used by primary school teachers to identify the 'prone' children:

1. Is he a nuisance, or does he take correction badly?
2. Has he been involved in wanton damage to property, truancy, or dishonest or other undesirable behaviour?
3. Does he choose as companions children who might lead him into such?
4. Is he untrustworthy or sly, so that it is hard to 'pin anything on him'?
5. Is he apt to be on bad terms with other children, or make himself disliked by bullying, spitefulness or underhand tricks?
6. Does he play to the gallery, show off, boast, or let himself be dared into foolish pranks?

One or more indications on this instrument would then justify more thorough examination, perhaps on a detailed adjustment guide, and a careful supportive policy towards the pupil from the beginning.

Whether pupils are troublesome because of marked and persisting maladjustment or because they come from homes with unsatisfactory standards of conduct and values, the long-term policies of schools are important in minimizing difficulties for individual teachers and in reducing both distress and subsequent severe sanctions for pupils. Clegg (1962) has emphasized the value of carefully thought out principles of conduct being uniformly applied throughout the school since these help greatly in avoiding situations conducive to troublesome behaviour, reducing the bullying, molestation and incitements to 'daring' which increase stress and provocation into foolish or delinquent acts. Here the general policy laid down by the headmaster in consultation with teachers can be decisive. Clegg cites a school in which troublesome behaviour flourished despite a great deal of physical punishment, but where a new headmaster over a space of five years reduced its delinquency rate to one of the lowest in the county – and did so with little use of corporal punishment. Early diagnosis and consistent school policy place considerable demands upon teachers, and it takes time for their effects to work through a school, but they provide two of the most effective counters against behaviour problems.

The Application of Motivation Study

A great deal of work is required in order to give an adequate account of the many aspects of pupil motivation. Some teachers are clearly more successful than others in stimulating high educational achievement, in getting exciting results even with pupils of limited abilities, and in creating good working conditions and relationships. However, it is often difficult to explain why or to give appropriate and systematic practical advice and training to beginners and the less successful. Up to a point we are able to draw attention to the important general principles of classroom motivation and to give evidence on practical policies and particular techniques which are effective or ineffective. The primary importance of intrinsic motivation and of acquired social motives for instruction and control is recognized. Associations can be demonstrated between particular patterns of teachers' behaviour and the responses generally made by pupils. The typical outcomes of particular techniques, such as teachers' sanctions, are established. And, we have a clearer picture of the role of school policies and of individual teachers in the reduction or development of troublesome behaviour. Indeed, at a general level we already possess the kinds of evidence necessary for producing sound and enlightened theories of instruction. Beyond this, however, much more information is needed for the effective translation of principles to the wide range of day-to-day situations in which teachers are placed; situations in which there are great variations in teachers, pupils and instructional objectives and contents. It would be very helpful if more work, oriented to practical situations, were available on the following matters to name but a few: the motivation of pupils from environments hostile or indifferent to school, especially at the crucial infant stage; the detailed programming of instruction for taking the greatest advantage of intrinsic motives; the consequences for pupils of the interaction between varied and distinctive teacher and pupil personalities; and the best ways of providing training in management skills for students who seem likely to have persistent disciplinary difficulties. It is in these areas that the criticism is sometimes made that, while the principles might be clear, teachers lack both detailed information and skills to put them into effective practice. However, it is not merely that research evidence is often lacking, for improved motivation also depends on teachers being willing to examine their own techniques and principles of instruction in the light of the information already available, and being prepared to modify their behaviour.

5 Communication and Assessment

Although a great deal of our time is spent with other people, the complicated nature of social and professional behaviour is often taken for granted. Only when something happens that is striking as a success or failure are we strongly prompted to ask ourselves why. In teaching it may be an outstanding lecture, the failure of an able pupil to make a success of a course, or a first lesson that goes badly. But after asking ourselves why, we are still likely to be left puzzled and uncertain. Part of the difficulty is the sheer rate and variety of interaction: in a few minutes in a classroom the teacher will have spoken to the class as a whole and to numerous individuals, each occasion bringing to bear different instructions, information and questions through a wide range of verbal and non-verbal techniques. In considering a brief episode, let alone a whole lesson or series of lessons, it is a major task to tease out even some of the specific acts, to relate these acts to pupils' responses or to determine whether they were relatively successful or not. One consequence is that research is limited. What has been done tends to be at the level of fairly general styles of communication or on the technical aspects of formal assessment of scholastic performance. Far less has been attempted on the analysis of specific kinds of verbal and non-verbal communication, on the acquisition of professional skills, and least of all on the complicated processes of impression formation and the development and influence of teachers' expectations for pupils.

This chapter attempts to go beyond the work on general teaching styles to look at some of the evidence currently available on more specific topics. To do so, it has been organized around two broad and related themes: *communication*, dealing with the verbal and non-verbal techniques of teachers, classroom communication struc-ture, and the methods used by teachers to influence the values and opinions of pupils; and *assessment*, dealing with teachers' assessments of the achievements and personal characteristics of pupils, the effects of increasing the teacher's information about his pupils, and the part played by teachers' expectations in influencing the educational responses of pupils. Finally, several of these topics are considered in relation to techniques of professional training.

Communication

Patterns of verbal behaviour

The teacher spends a great deal of his time in speaking to pupils: factual information, modes of analysis, concepts and values are presented, and in varying degrees influence the pupils' thinking, their attitudes and aspiration, and behaviour towards the teacher and one another. Skills, then, in the use of language are of profound importance.

Moving from one classroom to another it soon becomes apparent that patterns of verbal behaviour differ widely, but also that the individual teacher shows considerable consistency over a variety of teaching situations in the pattern he adopts. How great are the variations in verbal behaviour, and do particular patterns relate to pupils' achievements and class behaviour? Some of the most interesting studies have been done by Flanders (1960b) with teachers of mathematics and social studies in high schools. Using his systematic observation scheme, which we described earlier, observers categorized teacher and pupil verbal behaviour, then examined the data in relation to the achievements of pupils, their dependency behaviour, and attitudes to school.

The general pattern that emerged was that the largest number of entries was for lecturing, followed by the giving of directions and of criticism, and then by the acceptance of pupils' feelings, praise, questioning and the use of pupils' ideas. Lecturing, at some 25 per cent of the total time, was fairly stable over all teachers, but entries in the other categories varied widely, ranging from 12 per cent to 24 per cent for giving directions and criticism, and from 3 per cent to 8 per cent on accepting pupils' feelings, giving praise and using ideas. Correspondingly, pupils' verbal activity ranged between 20 per cent and 31 per cent for verbal responses to teachers, and between 14 per cent and 22 per cent on initiating communication with them.

Differences between teachers formed a basis for their classification as either 'indirect–expansive' or 'directive–restrictive', the former being those who made greater use of pupils' statements, clarification and expansion of ideas, extended questioning and acknowledgement of pupils' contributions. Indirect–expansive verbal behaviour was associated with significantly superior achievements of pupils in mathematics and social studies, with less pupil dependency upon the teacher and with more favourable school attitudes. However, some qualification needs to be made in order to bring out the particular value of this pattern. The point that Flanders makes is that indirect–expansive behaviour is most effective where it is used in the opening cycle of a lesson or in a new stage of lesson development, and then followed by the flexible use of both forms. The merit, then, lies not in a blanket adoption of one pattern but in appropriate application of one or the other at key points.

Logical behaviour of teachers

The most obvious functions of verbal communication in the classroom are to present information and to foster understanding in the various areas of the curriculum. For example, in teaching science we seek to give both an ordered description of phenomena and explanation, these involving definition, classification, hypothesizing, and the examination and evaluation of evidence from observation and experiment. It is commonly assumed that the logical characteristics of the teacher's exposition play a very important part in achieving these objectives; however, there is little information either on the actual behaviour of teachers or on its effects on pupils.

The initial problem here has been that of finding a suitable way of observing and categorizing what goes on. However, one study by Meux and Smith (1964) has tackled the immediate issue of what logical structure is revealed in particular episodes of teacher discourse by analysing the content into eleven categories of logical operations, such as defining, designating, classifying, evaluating and conditional inferring.

Their results indicate that teachers seldom conform to the structures expected in ideal forms of explanation, classification and so forth. Take, for example, a fairly common ideal form of explanation: something to be explained, an explanatory principle, and factual statements logically connecting the thing to be explained and the principle. However, in the classroom it is common to find explanations which either omit the connecting fact or the explanatory principle. Evaluation, which is an important aspect of all studies, and most obviously so with literary and historical work, is often defective. Here, four elements are involved: something to be evaluated, a criterion, facts about the thing to be evaluated which support the relevance of the criterion and finally a value rating. Yet the criterion is often not given, or the facts supporting its relevance are missing. Of course, there are many situations in the classroom where to spell out all the elements would be unnecessary in the light of facts, criteria and principles which are already established. Nevertheless, the case for careful study of how teachers handle these aspects of verbal behaviour is strong, since it may well be that teachers make too many assumptions about the background understanding of pupils and about their capacities to handle certain concepts and logical operations.

The importance of the last point comes out most clearly in the context of work on the cognitive development of pupils where the outstanding studies of Piaget (e.g.

Piaget, 1952; Piaget and Inhelder, 1956) map out major stages, broadly corresponding to chronological age, and therefore to school classes, in the ways young children and adolescents interpret their environments, handle concrete and symbolic material, and seek to solve problems. The subsequent application of his work to the curriculum, in such areas as the acquisition of mathematical concepts, of time and space concepts in history and geography, and of ideas of nationality and international relations, has given us a far greater appreciation of the capabilities of pupils, of the constraints upon them, and of the need to match curricular objectives and content to what can reasonably be expected of them. In some cases, as instanced by Goldman's work on religious thinking (1964), the evidence suggests that some syllabuses have contained conceptual material which required very skilful exposition by teachers, or should not have been there at all in view of the probable stage of cognitive development of the pupils being taught. Unfortunately our psychological knowledge of pupils is not matched by knowledge of the verbal skills required to foster the acquisition of understanding. An essential preliminary here is the descriptive analysis of the forms of exposition and questioning employed by teachers.

Modes of language in the classroom

In many of the professional encounters between adults the existence of common social backgrounds, educational experiences and interests makes it relatively easy for them to speak to one another in a language that has structure and content with which they are mutually familiar. Of course, situations can arise where communication breaks down, but explanations for this are likely to be found in perceptions of others, in conflicts over objectives, and in defects in organization structures. In the classroom, however, several factors exist which either singly or together can create great difficulties in the way of communication. Teachers and pupils are often widely separated in age, clearly very different in the extent of their social and educational experiences, and often from markedly different social backgrounds. Such differences can have the effect of producing classroom situations in which teachers and pupils have markedly little in the way of a common mode of language.

In Britain, Bernstein (e.g. 1961) has given particular attention to the analysis of social class differences in language and to the implications of the language environment for children's responses to education. The emphasis in this work has been upon the function of language as a representation of the ways individuals and groups organize their thought and their interpretation of the social environment. Two general forms of language have been posited: the 'restricted' and 'elaborated' codes. The elaborated code is characterized by grammatically complex sentence construction, accurate syntax, the frequent use of prepositions which indicate logical relations, a discriminative and broad use of adjectives and adverbs, and the frequent use of the personal pronoun 'I'. It is a mode of language designed for the detailed representation of past events and future plans, and for abstract and symbolic coding of experience. In contrast, the restricted code exhibits short, grammatically simple and often syntactically weak sentences; there is relatively little use of a range of adverbs or adjectives; subordinate clauses and impersonal pronouns are more infrequent; and there is the frequent supposition of prior mutual understanding, expressed in terms like 'you know' and 'you see'. Here, the language is largely limited to the function of handling social relations within situations of implicitly accepted common meanings and values.

A major problem in some classrooms is that of the teacher employing a language code to which the pupils have no equivalent response. Through his social and educational experiences and the nature of his professional material, he will use the elaborated code, whilst his pupils, if they come from backgrounds of impoverished language, will not. Where this happens the limitations

placed on communication can lead to unsatisfactory educational and control responses, and to a spiralling incomprehension that prevents the development of extensive
sequences of teacher–pupil verbal behaviour. The following illustration of conversation between a student teacher
and a pupil (Hannam *et al.*, 1968) brings out some of the
points raised.

Student: I see they have refused to sing for the Aberfan
disaster, the Beatles.
Pupil: Have they?
Student: What do you think about that?
Pupil: Well, it's all according to what …
Student: You think they should …
Pupil: Well, they sort of, you know, if they sang something,
you know, it could sort of, you know, bring, you
know, not be very nice if you know what I mean, you
know.
Student: You mean, if they sang something that isn't suitable,
you mean …
Pupil: Yes, yes.

In their everyday work many teachers are well aware of
the kind of problem described here and attempt to overcome it through more skilful methods than that shown by
the student above, especially by creating classroom
situations which encourage speaking by pupils and by
taking great care in framing the content and expression of
instruction. However, the origins of distinctive modes of
language and thought lie outside school and in the pre-
school experiences of children, and the school seems
unlikely to have any important influence unless it is
recognized at the infant beginnings of the careers of
children that some may require very skilful teaching directed at language development.

Classroom organization

So far the discussion of classroom communication has been
concerned with the personal skills and techniques of
teachers and we should now consider how various forms of

classroom organization may restrict or expand the number and effectiveness of channels of communication between teachers and pupils and between the pupils themselves.

Differences in teacher-imposed organization can readily be observed: one teacher will spend much of his time directing class activities from the desk area at the front of the class, with the pupils arranged in rows of desks before him; while in another classroom, the teacher will move about a great deal, working with individuals or small groups who are physically arranged about clusters of desks and work surfaces. These two broad structures, shown in Figure 8, present very different possibilities for communication. The first, called coaction by Olson (1957), shows communication largely restricted to a single channel between the teacher and his pupils, with the emphasis on the teacher initiating and controlling discourse and attempting to hold the attention of the whole class. The second pattern potentially has more channels: teacher to individual pupil and reverse, teacher to group and reverse, individuals to one another within a group, and cross group communication. There are, of course, many variations upon these structures and in the extent to which possible channels are utilized by teachers and pupils, and the possiblities are likely to be influenced by the nature of the subject being taught, the kinds of tasks to be undertaken and the basic design of the classroom.

The second pattern has become increasingly popular. It is now common in primary schools and more and more use of it can be expected at primary and secondary levels as new schools are designed with this end in view. This popularity stems from several sources: in the first instance, the relative informality of the arrangement is likely to reduce the feeling on the part of pupils that the teacher is someone quite separated from them both socially and as a contributor to the work they are doing; secondly, grouping serves not only to adjust work to the capacities of individuals but also provides circumstances in which group and individual self-control may supplement the influences

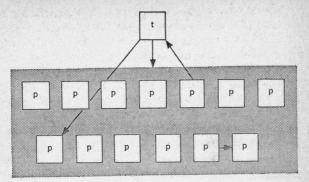

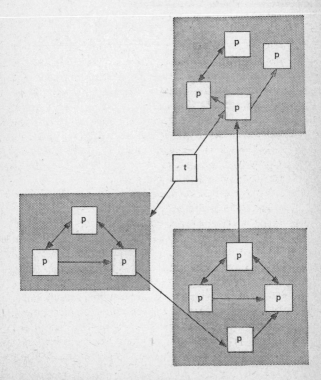

Figure 8. Communication structures

of the teacher; and, thirdly, the situation allows for many different activities to go on simultaneously, and for the teacher to distribute his attention as it may be required. However, enthusiasm and popularity are not in themselves sufficient grounds for adopting a particular arrangement, and the claims made for the superiority of the second pattern have not been clearly substantiated. Such evidence as there is indicates that the consistent use of one pattern is less effective than appropriate use of both, but the specification for when one or the other should be used is lacking. The lack of clear evidence on the merits of different forms of organization does not mean that there is little to choose between them; it can partly be explained by the failure of past research to agree on definitions of kinds of structures, to be clear about the criteria on which to evaluate them, and to take sufficient account of the characteristics of teachers in real situations. The personal preferences and organization skills of teachers seem particularly important in determining how effective a particular structuring will be. Study of the relatively simple coaction pattern indicates that teachers differ widely in their abilities to use even restricted channels of communication. Withall (1951) found, for example, that the distribution of attention to pupils can be highly distorted and that teachers can be quite ignorant of this. Thus, one teacher was found to be giving more than a quarter of his total attention to two well-adjusted pupils out of an entire class of twenty-six. Even after this had been pointed out to him, and he became concerned to produce a better distribution, he was only partly successful in his efforts. Taking this aspect alone, it seems likely that more complicated forms of organization would require relatively more skilful teacher behaviour. Furthermore, effective use of a large number of channels to different individuals and groups doing different tasks demands a degree of sensitivity to individual needs, qualities of basic organization of groups and tasks, and flexibility of control techniques which some teachers simply do not possess, either because of personal traits or because they lack the appropriate training and experience. Where these are lacking, ambitious attempts to produce a complicated structure may lead to deterioration of general supervision and particular groups and individuals may so lack guidance and attention that grouping becomes synonymous with shared ignorance.

Lectures and tutorials

In recent years a great deal of the work on class communication has been focused upon teaching practices in further and higher education. The particular issue here has been over the respective merits of lectures and discussion/ tutorial groups, and numerous studies have sought to compare them in terms of the achievements of students. McLeish (1966), examining the lecture method alone in terms of students' retention of content, found that there was immediate recall of up to 40 per cent of the material, but that this had dropped to some 15 per cent to 20 per cent a week later. Gauvain *et al.* (1965) compared postgraduate teaching by lecture or seminar, and here, seminars were regarded as less useful than lectures by the students, but there was no significant difference in the subsequent test scores from the two situations. In a study seeking evidence on the most efficient means of imparting information to medical students, Joyce and Weatherall (1957) compared the test scores on elementary statistics and psychopharmacology of students who had taken two-week courses either by lecture, discussion, practical classes or unsupervised reading. No significant differences between methods were found in the case of statistics, but in the other subject, methods were advantageous in the order: discussions, lectures, practicals and unsupervised reading. Also, students' preferences for methods were unrelated to subsequent performance. Such studies are individually interesting as observations on current techniques but it is not surprising to find many inconsistencies in comparative findings across the whole field. The situation closely resembles that found for classroom studies in schools, with the whole approach being so insensitive to the large individual variances arising from particular teachers, students, subjects and objectives that there seems little promise in pursuing this line of inquiry. In these circumstances, it would be more profitable to seek to characterize teacher competence within each major method, then to use this to guide training procedures towards the acquisition of particular management and social skills. As matters stand, vastly more effort is expended in arguments over the methods than in training people to use them well. A minority of our teachers in further and higher education have received professional teacher training, and even fewer, training which relates to the students and work of their institutions. A few universities have recognized this, and they provide voluntary short courses for young lecturers and for others who wish to get information on particular techniques, but the remainder must rely upon their own experiences as students and upon such general social skills as they may possess.

Non-verbal communication

Although the teacher's verbal behaviour is the most important and obvious aspect of his communication with pupils, the regulation of pupils' responses, especially in the area of classroom behaviour, and their perceptions of personality and emotional states, owe a great deal to non-verbal signals which, alone or in conjunction with speech, are rich in meaning. A glowering expression may do more than words to convey displeasure, to suggest further unpleasant consequences and to instigate a variety of actions by pupils.

Non-verbal communication stems from several sources: the teacher's posture, physical gestures, proximity to the pupil, eye contact, facial expressions, and non-linguistic aspects of speech. Each is important in itself, but in any individual the ways in which he integrates them give him a characteristic style by which he is recognized and responded to. However, beyond the general style, most people possess an extensive repertoire of sub-styles which they utilize in particular situations with the intention of achieving certain ends. This can be illustrated from findings, reported by Argyle (1967), on the use of eye contact. Looking at another person signals willingness to enter into a relationship and looking in return the readiness of the other to enter also. Looking indicates attitudes or emotions, with plentiful eye contact being used to show friendliness or willingness to prolong an encounter. Dropping of eye contact, coupled with an unfavourable facial expression, is used to show rejection of the other person.

Variations in physical proximity can be used to convey intimacy or the prestige of one person in relation to another. In the classroom the separation of the teacher from his pupils by a 'no man's land' between his desk and their seats has traditionally been used to indicate teacher authority and his role as arbiter of the behaviour of those in front of him. Not only has such isolation served to strengthen the demonstration of authority, but has limited intimacy, and by making the pupil leave his own territory for that of the teacher when called to discuss work or behaviour has put him at a disadvantage.

Commonly, non-verbal and verbal techniques are combined to reinforce one another in producing a particular outcome. Nodding of the head together with such expressions as 'yes' or 'uh huh' is frequently used to sustain an encounter, and it has been shown that by varying the amount of this pattern interviewers can regulate more or less eye contact and verbal responsiveness. However, skilled integration of verbal and non-verbal techniques is particularly hard for the teacher since the job requires him to be simultaneously affiliative and dominant. Too much dominance tends to produce either aggressiveness or over-submissiveness and passivity, whilst highly affiliative behaviour can lead to complete breakdown of control and refusal to work. Lacking experience in the appropriate balance required for the classroom, young teachers sometimes run into difficulties because they tend to emphasize the affiliative techniques which have been effective in their general interpersonal encounters with adults and friends. Their difficulties are further aggravated by, on the one hand, the fact that pupils of different ages and backgrounds are likely to respond best to rather different combinations of techniques, and, on the other, by the differences between schools in the general styles of influence to which pupils have become accustomed.

Failing systematic evidence upon the best techniques for particular situations, it is possible only to give the general opinions of teachers and pupils as to what is more or less effective and liked or disliked. In creating affiliation the following are important: close physical proximity, plenty of eye contact, smiling coupled with a pleasant appearance, and frequent agreement with the other person. Effectiveness in dominance also requires plenty of eye contact, together with a confident bearing, careful control of verbal exchanges, careful attention to what the other person says, and strong distinct speech. From pupils there is fairly general agreement on ineffective and disliked behaviour: inconsistency of the image presented, discouragement, lack of non-verbal reinforcement, sarcasm, ridicule, excessive self-reference and indistinct speech.

At present we are handicapped in teaching by the lack of detailed studies of techniques to be used at different stages in lessons and with pupils whose modes of communicating differ noticeably from those of the teacher. In general this is not the kind of work that can be done in the classroom itself, but requires controlled laboratory study of teacher–pupil pairs.

Influencing pupils' attitudes

The preceding discussion of communication in the classroom has concentrated upon the use of verbal and non-verbal techniques in relation to pupils' understanding and classroom behaviour. However, teachers have other, if less explicitly stated, objectives: they seek to present certain values, beliefs and practices to their pupils. These attempts to inform and influence extend to values, tastes and appreciation in art, music, literature, domestic design and fashion; to beliefs and evaluations of peoples, countries and policies through the teaching of history, geography and modern studies; and to the benefits of practices like dental care, non-smoking, sound diets and personal hygiene.

For two reasons it is difficult to write on these aspects of communication skills: in the first place, although an enormous amount of work has been done on attitude change most of it concerns adult subjects and situations other than the school, and there is regretably little research to tell us what long-term effects arise from schooling; and, in the second place, this is a very sensitive area in which ethical objections abound, so that techniques which are psychologically effective may very reasonably be rejected educationally. Regarding the first of these, it has been necessary to be rather selective of work which appears relevant to the classroom.

Three general techniques are available: exposure to information, to novel ways of bringing together diverse information and evaluating it; getting pupils to engage, by one means or another, in unaccustomed and perhaps initially disliked behaviours; and through deliberate and overt presentation of opinions which either had not occurred to pupils or run counter to those they already held. Within each of these procedures some or all of the following variables operate: the form of presentation of the communication, the perceived characteristics of the communicator, the degree to which an individual is made to commit himself to an opinion or behaviour contrary to his usual one, and the degree to which the personal characteristics of an individual lay him open more than others to persuasion.

In seeking to influence should the teacher present both sides of an argument or only the favourable one? Should he spell out his conclusions or leave it to the pupils to draw their own? Should he put his best arguments first or last, his favourable ones first or last? To answer these questions the teacher needs to know what opinions pupils already hold and how well informed they are on the subject of the communication – things of which he is commonly more or less ignorant. In general, putting both sides of a case is more effective with the better informed; drawing an explicit conclusion is preferable to leaving the issue open – especially since some pupils may miss the point altogether if this is not done; and strong and favourable arguments first is the appropriate order where the communication is coming from an authoritative source such as the teacher may be.

In framing the communication there is obviously a choice between the use of rational and emotionally fairly neutral appeals, and those which are couched in highly emotive terms. Appeals that stress the more alarming consequences of having certain opinions or of doing particular things are not uncommon in schools, yet it is doubtful whether they are more effective. Janis and Feshbach (1953) used three types of appeal with college students on the subject of dental hygiene, one containing information and illustration of high fear arousal content, a second containing information and illustration on milder consequences but omitting reference to the possible serious ones, and a third version which was more neutral and made fewer forecasts of frightening consequences of neglect of teeth. The effects of these messages were assessed in relation to the extent to which actual dental care practices changed and in the degree to which the students resisted counter arguments attempting to dismiss the original communications. Minimum fear arousal was the most effective in both respects: thus, although all three groups of students learned similar amounts of factual material the group exposed to the more fear arousing content appeared to ignore or minimize the importance of the threats.

When someone is attempting persuasion we should

expect that his hearers' perceptions of his credibility, his fairness and his motives for trying to influence them, and their feelings of liking or disliking towards him would all affect their responses. High school pupils in Kelman and Hovland's study (1953) showed changes in opinions about extreme leniency in the treatment of juvenile delinquency in order as the same communication came from 'a judge in a juvenile court', 'a randomly chosen member of a studio audience', and a 'member of a studio audience about whom indications were given that he had been a juvenile delinquent and was a criminal'. Other studies of credibility have considered the effects of perceived impartiality and perceptions of the communicator's motives in changing opinions. Various findings do suggest that aspects of credibility relate to acceptance of a communication; however, credibility variables do not appear to have persisting effects, so that differences between high and low credibility sources in bringing about changes in opinions tend to disappear over a few weeks (Hovland and Weiss, 1951). Nor, it should be added, does the credibility of the communicator show much influence upon the extent to which the content of the communication is learned.

One of the more important factors influencing acceptance of a particular opinion or behaviour is public commitment. Classrooms potentially offer highly appropriate situations for taking advantage of commitment techniques since they contain peer groups whose opinions are likely to matter a great deal to the particular individuals in the classes. Teachers may therefore be able to use their communication skills to bring out opinions that are commonly held throughout the group, and to get particular pupils to express similar opinions although these may be contrary to those previously held. Furthermore, through their organization of classroom activities, teachers can get pupils to commit themselves publicly in role-playing and written work. Success in using such procedures not only depends upon skilful verbal behaviour on the part of teachers but also upon their knowledge of the motivations and relationships of pupils, and abilities in class management.

In addition to teachers' skills in communicating and pupils' perceptions of teachers and situations, the extent of influence achieved is affected also by the personality characteristics of the hearers. Individuals' needs for information, for confirmation, for recognition, or for opportunities to project personal impulses upon others, provide communicators – especially the more unscrupulous – with powerful allies. Thus, pupils who are themselves highly aggressive are likely to be more willing to accept communications which advocate aggressive and punitive attitudes towards others. Those who are socially isolated, low in self-esteem, or over-sensitive to the opinions of others rather than being self-directed, are more susceptible. Compliance and possibly acceptance too, are related to sex. Women students in teacher training (Morrison and McIntyre, 1967) showed greater shifts in educational opinions over a year than did men, with correspondingly greater reversals during the following year of teaching. Finally, studies of influence upon the same individuals over several situations suggest a general trait of persuasibility.

With so many factors to take into account, teachers need to be well informed about the information, opinions and personality characteristics of their pupils in deciding upon appropriate and acceptable ways of influencing them. It is simply not sufficient to 'off-load' information, lay down the 'right' opinions, or force superficial compliance, and then hope for the best. Although general studies of attitude change can be useful guides we urgently need more evidence from schools on the influence of teachers, especially against the background of other influences. It is quite remarkable that such strong views should be held on the influence teachers should have, and what is permissible or not, and yet in reality for so little to be known.

Assessment

Mention of assessment in the classroom conjures up a picture of pupils labouring over tests and written exercises, and of teachers spending long hours in compiling questions in marking, and in producing sets of marks and individual reports. Assessment in this sense is, of course, a basic part of the teacher's work, but only a small part of the total search for information about pupils is of this formal kind. In the field of scholastic achievement alone most of the information sought by teachers comes from fairly informal procedures of observation and questioning. To begin with, then, we should recognize that our understanding of assessment in the classroom, and of how teachers might improve some of their practices can be helped only in a limited way by reference to the extensive work that has been done on the formal and external examining of educational achievement. Secondly, although scholastic assessment is a dominant concern, teachers spend a far greater proportion of their time observing, evaluating and acting upon indications of ongoing social behaviour and upon forming impressions of the more or less persisting personal traits of pupils. Virtually all of this is done informally and so taken for granted that there is little conscious awareness of doing so. Finally, although assessment is used most obviously as a means to give teachers scholastic information on their pupils it has two other important uses in the classroom, namely, to provide them with checks upon their own performances, and to give pupils comparative information on their behaviour.

Clearly, to consider only formal scholastic assessment hardly does justice to the range of the subject or to the complexity of the processes involved. This point can be illustrated by taking one of the several schemes which have been suggested for describing information processing by teachers in the classroom. Ryans (1963) identifies five phases: (a) sensing, identifying and classifying inputs;

(b) evaluation of possible courses of action; (c) making of decisions by the teacher; (d) programming or logical-psychological ordering and arranging of output; (e) transmission of appropriate information to the pupil. This scheme can readily be applied to scholastic assessment and, if this done, then it is not too difficult to recognize the kinds of technical and evaluative problems that arise and to see how, at least partly, they might be overcome. But, for the non-scholastic aspects of pupils, usually more informally assessed, the whole process becomes enormously complicated by the diversity of available information, the variations in the range and reliability of the cues provided by pupils, and most of all, by the sheer difficulty of distinguishing from one another the effects of teachers' characteristics, the perceived characteristics of pupils, and pupils' perceptions of and responses to teachers.

Looked at in these various ways, assessment raises a range of issues, some of which have hardly been touched upon in research on teachers' behaviour. As instances, what are the basic features of teachers' assessment procedures, what part is played by their expectations of pupils in regulating achievements and social behaviour, and how can teachers be trained more effectively in the various kinds of assessment skills?

Teachers' ratings of pupils

How do teachers categorize the attributes of their pupils, and how are the categories ordered in terms of interest to them? Several studies of teachers' ratings of the personality traits and attainments of pupils (e.g. Hallworth, 1962) show that teachers in British schools are generally consistent in discriminating three clusters of characteristics. The first cluster concerns pupil attainment. In effect, the teacher is asking 'how well does this pupil get on with schoolwork?' and attention is centred upon general ability, and performance in such subjects as English and arithmetic. The characteristics forming the second cluster bear particularly upon general classroom behaviour and attitudes to teachers: courtesy, cooperation with teachers, trustworthiness, persistence and attentiveness – 'how well do I get on with this pupil?' The third cluster of correlations typically includes cheerfulness, leadership, popularity, social confidence and co-operation with other pupils, and appears to represent an assessment of social traits which relate particularly to the teacher's perception of how well a pupil is getting on with other pupils.

This assessment pattern is common to teachers in primary and secondary schools, but undergoes interesting modifications in relation to particular environments, and to differences in age, sex and educational attitudes of teachers (McIntyre, Morrison and Sutherland, 1966). Men and women, those working with pupils from working class backgrounds and from middle class backgrounds, differ in the extent to which their ratings of attainment are independent of ratings of classroom behaviour. Teachers tend to make a more uniform generalized assessment of a girl than they do of a boy; younger teachers show more concern with classroom behaviour and older teachers with attainment; the 'tough-minded' teacher stresses 'quietness' as a major characteristic of the behaviour of a pupil who gets on well with him; and particular interests of some teachers may be reflected in the use of a single trait category, as is the case for male primary school teachers making ratings of 'games ability' of boys.

Such differences in perception probably reflect important variations in the teacher's search for information, in his sensitivity to particular characteristics, and in his use of stereotypes. Furthermore, these perceptual variations almost certainly lead to more or less subtle differences in behaviour towards individuals and groups, although we have little systematic evidence on this.

A general impression of the order of teachers' interest in aspects of their pupils can be obtained in another way. Table 4 gives the results obtained by the present writers from a study of primary school teachers, the teachers having been asked to rank characteristics according to the number of occasions on which they found themselves discussing particular aspects of pupils.

Table 4 Aspects of Pupils Most Discussed by Their Teachers[1]

Characteristic	Ranking by frequency	Total of ranks
General ability	1	231
Carelessness	2	343
Laziness	3	463
Talkativeness	4	485
Cooperativeness	5	552
Persistence	6	638
Courtesy	7	642
Ability to use language	8	672
Originality	9	717

1. A high rank indicates high frequency. The total number of teachers was fifty-six.

This extract shows only those characteristics which preoccupy teachers, namely the pupils' scholastic performance and general classroom behaviour; if the rankings are continued then we find that such social traits as social confidence, sociability and popularity come very near to the bottom of their list.

Assessment procedures

Professional interest in assessing scholastic performance has had several consequences. It has the effect of ensuring that there is regular and systematic assessment of all pupils through formal testing and exercises, and through questioning, so that teachers soon acquire a great deal of comparative and individual information which they can put to use in deciding upon patterns of class and individual instruction and in devising remedial work. Furthermore, it has stimulated a great deal of work on the development of sound techniques for a wide range of assessment purposes, and on the use of assessment programmes. When it is also taken into account that teachers themselves are relatively expert in academic fields, then on all these grounds we can expect that they will be more competent assessors of scholastic performance than of other aspects of their pupils.

Nevertheless, shortcomings can exist. The very confidence that some teachers have in their abilities gives them excessive faith in the quality of their measures and evaluations. This can lead in turn to failure to recognize major sources of error affecting evaluations of pupils' work and to faulty conclusions about the extent and nature of difficulties being experienced by individual pupils. Secondly, their assessment procedures are sometimes tacked on to the end of a piece of teaching, like obituaries on instruction, rather than forming a carefully constructed complement to it. Much of the difficulty here arises from teachers failing to be clear in their own minds about their educational objectives and therefore not being in the position to determine a really appropriate means of assessment. Looking at many class tests and exercises it is often difficult to decide either what they are supposed to tell us about the pupil or whether what they can tell us has any relation to the instruction given. And, finally, the confidence of teachers is most suspect regarding their skills in informal assessment through questioning and the use of non-verbal cues. On this last point, for example, teachers must rely to some extent upon cues indicating understanding or incomprehension in deciding whether to continue to the next stage or to go over ground again with further teaching and questioning. Getting this feel of how pupils are responding is very important, yet teachers vary very much in their sensitivity to these cues.

Earlier it was suggested that the processes concerned with observation and evaluation of pupils' immediate behaviour, personality and social relationships were particularly difficult to examine. Studies on the formation of impressions of personality provide some pointers here (Asch, 1946; Bruner *et al.*, 1958). We all enter into encounters with others with an implicit personality theory about the structure of personal attributes. Several consequences arise from this: one is that the characteristics we attribute to others are the products of such 'objective' characteristics as others possess and the expectations we bring to the situation on the basis of our theories; another is that such theories provide us with a ready made set of correlations, so that given even very limited information on one aspect of another person we are prepared to go beyond the information given to a set of inferences about him which have high subjective probability. Thus, the impressions we form depend, among other things, upon:

1. The patterns of inferences we are accustomed to make.

2. Our personal tendencies towards either moderate or extreme judgements about the attributes of others.

3. The choice of the salient traits from which we build up the general impression.

4. The sensitivity we possess towards particular observational cues or classes of cues – voice, physical features, movement, and so on.

Given, then, a teacher and some twenty to forty pupils, what are some of the likely features of the teacher's 'search' for information? Perhaps the most obvious is that the sheer amount of information actually or potentially available will be enormous, and the teacher's capacity for handling it relatively so limited that he will have to be selective. In practice, this may mean concentrating his attentions on particular characteristics and individuals, for example, the pupils who are the ablest and poorest performers, and those who are the most troublesome or the best behaved. What he selects is also likely to be influenced by the availability of cues, for some areas of behaviour and traits are open to him while others are less so and may even be concealed by pupils. These limitations, coupled with his own expectations and manner of perceiving pupils, will determine the final form of the search made, the evaluations he arrives at, and the behaviour that follows.

In these circumstances individuals are going to differ a great deal in the skills they possess. An interesting illustration can be taken from teachers' assessments of the peer group relations of pupils. This is a matter of some importance since pupils low in acceptance may reflect this in lack of interest in schoolwork or poor behaviour, whilst those high in status can exert considerable influence upon the behaviour of others. Either way, relationships between pupils affect the teacher. But teachers are commonly uninterested in these relationships and pupils don't readily reveal this side of themselves. The result, as several studies comparing teachers' assessments with those of pupils have shown, is that teachers are often very poor judges of the actual state of affairs. Not only do they make errors about individuals, but they can fail to recognize even the most general patterns of preferences (Blyth, 1958). Two main sources of error exist. The first, in this area of very limited cues, is that teachers may misinterpret what they see and hear. Pupils who are observed to be socially highly active, mixing with many others on apparently very good terms, may be judged as highly popular, although the observed activity may represent unsuccessful attempts to establish a relationship of any sort, and particularly with a high prestige individual who will tolerate a lot of hangers on. Manifest social activity is an ambiguous cue, likely to mislead about the low status pupil, and the reserved and relatively inactive child who has qualities which make him highly influential. The second source lies in the patterns of correlations and inferences mentioned earlier. Within a cluster a favourable rating on one trait predicts a parallel rating on another. If the teacher assesses a pupil as high on social confidence then he is likely to do so for leadership, cheerfulness, co-operation with other pupils, and popularity. To a lesser extent, similar levels of rating run right across the range of pupils' characteristics so that those who are regarded by the teacher as cooperative and attentive tend to be over-estimated on peer relationships, whilst those who are uncooperative tend to be underestimated. Some of the difficulties in the selection and interpretation of cues in this area are discussed by Bonney (1947). However, the points raised here have wide implication for teachers' skills across the whole range of behaviour and scholastic assessment.

Effects of increasing information

One way of looking at the possibilities for improving class-room assessment and subsequently instruction itself is in terms of the information available on pupils. What happens then when the amount of information is increased? Does it improve the teacher's assessment, and does it affect his behaviour and that of the pupils? In a study of the achievements and attitudes of sixteen-year-olds, Ojemann and Wilkinson (1939) examined the effects of giving teachers supplementary information on their pupils. They took two groups of pupils matched on age, present achievement and intelligence, and collected information of a detailed kind not normally available to teachers on the pupils' personality characteristics, personal problems and home backgrounds. For the experimental group, this additional information, together with suggestions as to its uses and meaning, was given to the teachers at the beginning of the school year. Both groups were tested on achievements and school attitudes at the beginning and again nine months later. Comparisons between the two groups at the end of the experiment indicated significantly greater achievement gain, more favourable school attitudes and also fewer indications of

personality conflict for the pupils of the more fully informed teachers. Some of the teachers' observations are
interesting:

'After your account of L.M. I see her as an unhappy child
rather than an insolent one. I find it easier to accept her.'

'After discovering it was shyness and nervousness rather
than sulkiness which prevented L.C. from reciting, I made a
special effort to see what could be done to help him overcome
this difficulty. I seated him so that he could be centrally located,
praised him at every reasonable opportunity, encouraged him
not to do things alone but in company with his classmates. . . .'

'After learning that she received so little encouragement
at home I endeavoured to praise her school work at every
opportunity that arises. . . .'

Information and self-evaluation

A further important way in which information supply
affects classroom situations is in changing self-evaluations
of teachers and pupils. Most of us are curious to know what
others think of us. We want to know how well we are
getting on in tasks and what personal impressions we have
created. Part of the search for information is for such
evaluation, and what we discover can have powerful effects
on subsequent behaviour.

It is difficult for teachers to know how they are behaving.
Self-images may be poles apart from the impressions
formed by pupils and despite their best intentions they
may persist in unsuitable behaviours for want of external
evidence. The main difficulty is that the rules of the
classroom game normally prevent them from getting the
information from those who have it – the pupils. They
cannot ask, nor can the pupils tell. This is unfortunate
since what pupils might have to say could benefit teachers
and eventually themselves. Gage *et al.* (1960) have demonstrated this experimentally by breaking the rules. They
obtained the opinions of pupils on twelve aspects of their
teachers' behaviour, such as, 'acts disappointed when a
pupil gets something wrong', 'explains arithmetic so

pupils can understand it', and 'enjoys a funny remark made by a pupil', then presented the information to the teachers. Subsequent testing indicated changes in teachers' behaviour on ten of the twelve dimensions. This feedback also produced improvement in the accuracy of teachers' perceptions of their pupils' opinions.

While few teachers will have the courage to follow Gage's ingenious procedures in their classrooms, they certainly are able to take advantage of the findings from the next study by Page (1958) concerning the pupils themselves. Pupils, of course, rarely lack advice from teachers on their behaviour; what they sometimes do lack is information that will tell them how well they are working. Some teachers use assessments largely for their own ends and neglect to feedback the results to pupils. Too often tests and exercises are returned to them with virtually meaningless ticks, crosses or marks. This is a gross waste of an important opportunity for motivation. Page sought to establish whether commenting on pupils' work was worth the effort, and if so, what form of comment was superior. Teachers administered objective tests to their classes which were then scored and graded before being randomly assigned to three treatment groups: no comment, free comment (whatever the teacher felt appropriate) and specified comment (a uniform comment thought to be generally encouraging). Tests were then returned to the students. Subsequent test performance of students indicated that free comment was superior to specified comment, and that to no comment at all. Furthermore, this was a consistent finding over the twelve schools and all the age groups tested. Since teachers often believe that it is worth while to comment on the work of better pupils, but rather a waste of time with the poorer, it is interesting to note that Page found no support for this point of view.

Teachers' assessments often get back to pupils in the form of test scores. Pickup and Anthony (1968) found that high-scoring pupils seemed to perform better if their scores had been lower than expected; however, low-scoring pupils, who usually received scores lower than those they had expected, performed better when they had received scores higher than they expected.

Teachers' expectations of pupils

Expectations are brought to the classroom or are very quickly acquired. Student teachers asked to write personality sketches of children, based upon a set of five sketch facts, and then to rate their 'children' on a variety of characteristics, commonly produce quite distinctive patterns of ratings according to whether one of the basic facts describes them as coming from a city tenement or privately owned housing background. The urban working-class children are more frequently described as having few interests, lacking in manners, poor leaders, showing little interest in school, being indifferent to success, and performing relatively poorly in schoolwork. Rough generalizations of what pupils can be expected to be like may be present, then, before the teacher enters service. Other factors also influence expectations. Anastasiow (1964) found that teachers perceived their classes' mean reading levels to be at the class grade level, regardless of actual reading achievement. A third grade (eight to nine year olds) teacher assigned the reading texts regarded as appropriate to this grade to her median pupils, even though these pupils were actually reading at the level of grade six. The interaction of teacher characteristics and pupil background may influence not only perceptions of pupils but also explanations as to why the pupils create teaching problems. Gottlieb (1964) found significant differences between white and Negro teachers in attitudes towards pupils of both races from low income families, white teachers describing them as 'talkative, lazy, fun loving, high strung and rebellious' and blaming parents and children for teaching problems, and Negro teachers describing them as 'fun loving, happy, cooperative, energetic and ambitious' and blaming the physical environment for problems.

How important are the teacher's expectations for his pupils? Perhaps some pupils do poorly in school because that is what is expected of them. Perhaps terms like 'working class' or 'disadvantaged' evoke anticipations of poor performance, setting up the conditions in schools and classrooms which confirm the expectation, teachers and pupils becoming enmeshed in circumstances from which they find it difficult to escape.

The important test would be to see what happens when teachers' expectations are altered, doing so in controlled circumstances to ensure that expectations are not contaminated by knowledge of the past performance of pupils, and also that the measures of subsequent performance in the 'new expectations' situation reflect actual behaviour and not just changed perceptions of the pupils by the teachers. Rosenthal and Jacobson (1968) have produced particularly interesting findings in such situations. The subjects were children in five grades of an elementary school, situated in a declining area of an American city, and drawing in children from middle and lower class families, the latter including families receiving welfare payments and Mexican–Americans. Teachers were told that the school was to help in the development of a new kind of verbal ability and reasoning test for predicting the intellectual gains in children, and this test material, in fact an established test, was administered to all the pupils. Four months later at the beginning of the new session, and when children had moved into their next grade classes, one in five of the children were chosen randomly by the experimenters, designated as 'spurters' who would show unusual intellectual gain, and their names then conveyed casually to their respective grade teachers at a pre-session staff meeting with the remark, 'by the way, in case you are interested in who did what in those tests we were doing for Harvard. . .'. Thus, the treatment of the 'spurters' was nothing more than giving their names to their new teachers as those who should do well. All the control and experimental children were subsequently retested at inter-

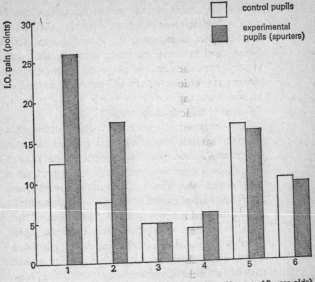

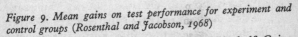

Figure 9. Mean gains on test performance for experiment and control groups (Rosenthal and Jacobson, 1968)

vals of several months over the next year and a half. Gains in test performance for the experimental 'spurters' and the controls in the different grades are shown in Figure 9.

In the first place, many children for whom teachers expected greater intellectual gains showed such gains. Among the younger groups the mean gains of 'spurters' were much greater than those of the control pupils. Secondly, when, at the end of the session, teachers were asked to describe the classroom behaviour of all children, the 'spurters' were described as being happier, more curious and more interesting than the other children. Also, they tended to perceive them as more appealing, more affectionate, less in need of social approval, and as having a better chance of success in later life. Thirdly, many of the control children also, of course, made gains, but the more they gained the less favourably they were rated on behaviour. This was most noticeable for the control children who made the most gains in the lowest ability 'track' in each grade. It seems, say the authors, 'difficult for a slow track child, even if his I.Q. is rising, to be seen by his teacher as a well adjusted and potentially successful student.'

These results do not seem explicable in terms of changed amounts of attention being given to the designated children, nor was there special provision of expensive equipment. Teaching methods remained unchanged and there were no special cultural programmes laid on. Whatever took place seems to have been in more subtle modifications of interpersonal behaviour. It appears that changed expectations can have impressive consequences not only for individuals but whole groups. Furthermore, the authors point out that the effects achieved in this way may be considerably greater than those coming from elaborate 'enrichment' programmes which are often based upon the assumption that the failings of pupils are inherent in themselves and their situations alone.

From the point of view of assessment these results are important in at least three ways. Firstly, it is evident that a source of information provided from outside the classroom can be a powerful corrective to teachers' personal evaluations of pupils – in this case even a false hint was sufficient! Secondly, without some external reference, teachers' assessments may form part of a confirmation process rather than means to the better understanding of pupils' capabilities or difficulties, a potential depresser rather than a stimulator of performance. Lastly, there are no neat and specific consequences from the teacher discovering something new about his pupils; rather there are multiple effects upon himself and them.

Training in Skills

Many teachers could benefit from a greater understanding of the technical and psychological aspects of classroom communication and assessment. The most obvious time to begin is during professional training where all could be given basic instruction and experience. The difficulties, however, are considerable when we often do not know what is susceptible to training, what methods are most effective, and what ground we should attempt to cover. Existing studies do help in some respects. They indicate that such general features of teachers as their verbal styles, distribution of attention and characteristic behaviours towards children can be considerably modified by deliberate procedures, for example, by the use of audiovisual feedback and discussion of the recorded behaviour rather than by good advice in lectures. Work by Gage *et al.* (1960) and Withall (1951) on modifying particular aspects of teachers has already been mentioned; in addition, Ishler (1967) has shown how effective professional feedback from a student supervisor can be in modifying verbal behaviour. Two groups of students, one serving as a control, were rated once a week over eleven weeks on Withall's Social-Emotional Climate Index. The experimental group was regularly given information on their verbal behaviour as recorded by the Index. Whilst verbal behaviour in both groups shifted significantly towards a learner-centred style, this was more pronounced for the experimental group.

The importance of skilful use of cues came out earlier in connexion with teachers' judgements of peer group status. Some improvement in this and other areas might come from direct instruction on techniques for observing others and from knowledge of simple questionnaire procedures such as sociometric tests, but telling students what happens and what they might do is no guarantee that they will put advice into practice. Sometimes direct training can be effective. Jecker *et al.* (1964), for instance, has shown that teachers can be trained to perceive more accurately whether pupils have understood what they have been taught. Teachers were shown brief films of children (separately from the films there was information available on whether pupils had understood) and their attention was drawn to the facial cues of comprehension. In this way it was possible to increase teachers' accuracy on a similar set of films.

Training can also increase the relevance and range of the student-teacher's ways of looking at classroom problems. Runkel and Damrin (1961) gave students a number of problems and asked them to say what information they would require in solving them and what they considered to be the order of importance of different types of information. In this way it was possible to establish the relevance and range of their ways of considering problems at the beginning of training, mid-way and near the end of the course. Students began with a large number of relevant and irrelevant ways, reducing them during the first part of training and then moving to a more complex and relevant position, with the most successful students tending to show the most marked variations from one position to another.

Probably a great deal could be done to improve techniques of formal assessment in scholastic areas through direct instruction in sound methods, through practical sessions on test construction, and by drawing students' attention to the proper functions of assessment within the curriculum. Although these seem obvious enough suggestions, it is still the case that some training courses fail to provide systematic instruction on educational assessment.

Conclusion

While it is obvious that appropriate training in social skills would be of great value to particular groups of teachers, such as those who have difficulty with classroom control, the evidence reviewed in this chapter shows that there is considerable scope for improvement on a more general scale. Much might already be done to increase specific teaching skills by the use of deliberate training procedures. Much more might be possible if the necessary research were undertaken: the systematic description of teachers' classroom behaviour; the identification of those skills which are most important for teachers and those with which they have greatest difficulty; the development of reliable procedures for assessing these skills; and controlled experiments with possible training methods, such as those mentioned in chapter 2.

However, as we have suggested earlier, professional training owes as much to traditional rituals, untested assumptions and dubious criteria as to policies based upon systematic study of teaching skills. This state of affairs is due both to the lack of research evidence and to a common belief that research is unnecessary and irrelevant. Thus not only is there a lack of facilities and staff for research, particularly research into teacher behaviour and training, but also a wide disregard for the results of research which is done.

This state of affairs in teacher training is paralleled in most sectors of the education system. Debates between traditionalists and supporters of current fashions are often carried on with none of the protagonists apparently feeling any need for scientific evidence. And among teachers, particularly in secondary and post-secondary education, respect and promotion are often awarded more in accordance with academic qualifications than with level of teaching skills. Among the most necessary conditions for educational advance are that teachers should pride themselves more on their mastery of the complex social and intellectual skills required for their work, and that such pride should be justified by the profession being based upon scientific research.

References

Altmann, E. (1967), 'The mature student teacher', *New Society*, 28 December.

American Educational Research Association (1952), 'Committee on the criteria of teacher effectiveness. Report of the Committee', *Rev. educ. Res.*, vol. 22, pp. 238–63.

Anastasiow, N. J. (1964), 'Frame of reference of teachers' judgements: the psychophysical model applied to education', *Psychology in Schools*, vol. 1, pp. 392–5.

Anderson, R. C. (1959), 'Learning in discussions: a resumé of the authoritarian-democratic studies', *Harvar educ. Rev.*, vol. 29, pp. 201–15.

Argyle, M. (1967), *The Psychology of Interpersonal Behaviour*, Penguin Books.

Asch, S. E. (1946), 'Forming impressions of personality', *J. abnorm. soc. Psychol.*, vol. 41, pp. 258–90.

Asch, S. E. (1951), 'Effects of group pressure upon the modification and distortion of judgement', in Guetzkow, H. (ed.), *Groups, Leadership, and Men*, Carnegie Press.

Ashley, B., Cohen, H., and Slatter, R. (1967a), 'Social classifications: relevance to the teacher', *Times Educational Supplement* (Scotland), 17 March.

Ashley, B., Cohen, H., and Slatter, R. (1967b), 'Why we are teachers', *Times Educational Supplement* (Scotland), 12 May.

Bach. J. O. (1952), 'Practice teaching success in relation to other measures of teaching ability', *J. exp. Educ.*, vol. 21, pp. 57–80.

Bandura, A., and Walters, R. H. (1965), *Social Learning and Personality Development*, Holt, Rinehart and Winston.

Becker, H. S. (1952), 'The career of the Chicago public schoolteacher', *Amer. J. Sociol.*, vol. 57, pp. 470–77.

Bellak, A. A. (1966), *The Language of the Classroom*, Teachers College Press, Columbia University.

Bernstein, B. (1961), 'Social structure, language and learning', *Educ. Res.*, vol. 3, pp. 163-76.

Biddle, B. J., Rosencranz, H. A., and Rankin, E. F. (1961), *Studies in the Role of the Public School Teacher*, University of Missouri Press, vols. 1-5.

Biddle, B. J., Rosencranz, H. A., Tomich, E., and Twyman, J. P. (1966), 'Shared inaccuracies in the role of the teacher', in Biddle, B. J., and Thomas, E. J. (eds.), *Role Theory: Concepts and Research*, Wiley.

Bloom, B. S., Engelhart, M. D., Furst, E. J., Hill, W. H., and Krathwohl, D. R. (1956, 1964), *Taxonomy of Educational Objectives: The Classification of Educational Goals*, Handbook 1: *Cognitive Domain; Handbook* 2: *Affective Domain*, Longmans.

Blyth, W. A. L. (1958), 'Sociometry, prefects and peaceful coexistence in a junior school', *Sociol. Rev.*, vol. 6, pp. 5-24.

Bogen, I. (1954), 'Pupil-teacher rapport and the teacher's awareness of status structures within the group', *J. educ. Sociol.*, vol. 28, pp. 105-14.

Bonney, M. (1947), 'Sociometric study of agreement between teachers' judgements and student choices', *Sociometry*, vol. 10, pp. 133-46.

Bovard, E. W. (1956), 'Interaction and attraction to the group', *Human Relations*, vol. 9, pp. 481-9.

Bruckman, I. R. (1966), 'The relationship between achievement motivation and sex, age, social class, school stream and intelligence', *Brit. J. soc. clin. Psychol.*, vol. 5, pp. 211-20.

Bruner, J. S. (1966), *Towards a Theory of Instruction*, Harvard University Press.

Bruner, J. S., Shapiro, D., and Tagiuri, R. (1958), 'The meaning of traits in isolation and in combination', in Tagiuri, R., and Petrullo, L. (eds.), *Person Perception and Interpersonal Behaviour* Stanford University Press.

Bryan, J. H. (1968), *Actions Speak Louder than Words: Model Inconsistency and its Effect on Self-Sacrifice*, Educational Testing Service, Princeton, New Jersey.

Butcher, H. J. (1965), 'The attitudes of student teachers to education', *Brit. J. soc. clin. Psychol.*, vol. 4, pp. 17–24.

Callis, R. (1950), 'Change in teacher–pupil attitudes related to training and experience', *Educ. psychol. Measmt*, vol. 10, pp. 718–27.

Children and their Primary Schools (1967), *A Report of the Central Advisory Council for Education (England)*, H.M.S.O., vol. 2. (Plowden Report)

Clark, R. P., and Nisbet, J. D. (1963), 'The first two years of teaching', Mimeographed report, Aberdeen College of Education.

Clegg, A. B. (1962), 'The role of the school', in *Delinquency and Discipline*, Councils and Education Press, London.

Cohen, L. (1967), 'The teacher's role as liaison between school and neighbourhood', in Croft, M., Raynor, J., and Cohen, L. (eds.), *Linking Home and School*, Longmans.

Collins, M. (1964), 'Untrained and trained graduate teachers: a comparison of their experiences during the probationary year', *Brit. J. educ. Psychol.*, vol. 34, pp. 75–84.

Cook, W. W., Leeds, C. H., and Callis, R. (1951), *Minnesota Teacher Attitude Inventory*, Psychological Corporation, New York.

Cornwell, J. (1958), 'Sociometric analysis in a residential training college', Unpublished Ph.D. Thesis, University of London.

Craig, H. (1960), 'The teacher's function: some observations on an aspect of the teacher's job in Scotland', *J. educ. Sociol.*, vol. 34, pp. 7–16.

Crutchfield, R. S. (1966), 'Creative thinking in children', in Brim, O. G., Crutchfield, R. S., and Holtzman, W. H. (eds.), *Intelligence Perspectives 1965*, Harcourt, Brace and World.

Deutsch, M. (1960), 'The effects of co-operation and competition upon group process', in Cartwright, D., and Zander, A. (eds.), *Group Dynamics: Research and Theory*, Row, Peterson.

Dickson, G. (1965), *The Characteristics of Teacher Education Students in the British Isles and the United States*, Research Foundation of the University of Toledo.

Douglas, J. W. B. (1964), *The Home and the School*, MacGibbon and Kee.

Entwhistle, N. J. (1968), 'Academic motivation and school attainment', *Brit. J. educ. Psychol.*, vol. 38, pp. 181–8.

Evans. D. (1967), 'The effects of achievement motivation and ability upon discovery learning and accompanying incidental learning under two conditions of incentive set', *J. educ. Res.*, vol. 60(5), pp. 195–200.

Evans, K. M. (1952), 'A study of attitudes towards teaching as a career', *Brit. J. educ. Psychol.*, vol. 32, pp. 63–9.

Evans, K. M. (1962), *Sociometry and Education*, Routledge and Kegan Paul.

Evans, K. M. (1967), 'Teacher training courses and students' personal qualities', *Educ. Res.*, vol. 10 (1), pp. 72–7.

Festinger, L. (1957), *A Theory of Cognitive Dissonance*, Row, Peterson.

Finlayson, D. S., and Cohen, L. (1967), 'The teacher's role: a comparative study of the conceptions of college of education students and head teachers', *Brit. J. educ. Psychol.*, vol. 37, pp. 22–31.

Flanders, N. A. (1960a), 'Interaction analysis in the classroom: a manual for observers', Unpublished manuscript, University of Michigan.

Flanders, N. A. (1960b), *Teacher Influence, Pupil Attitudes and Achievement*, Final Report, Co-operative Research Project No. 397, University of Minnesota.

Flanders, N. A. (1963), 'Intent, action and feedback: a preparation for teaching', in Silberman, H. F. (ed.), *A Symposium on Current Research on Classroom Behaviour* of Teachers and its Implications for Teacher Education, *J. teacher Educ.*, vol. 14 (September), pp. 251–60.

Flanders, N. A. (1964), 'Some relationships among teacher influence, pupil attitudes, and achievement', in Biddle, B. J., and Elena, W. J. (eds.), *Contemporary Research on Teacher Effectiveness*, Holt, Rinehart and Winston.

Flavell, J. H. (1963), *The Developmental Psychology of Jean Piaget*, Van Nostrand.

Gage, N. L., Runkel, P. J., and Chatterjee, B. B. (1960), *Equilibrium Theory and Behaviour Change: An Experiment in Feedback from Pupils to Teachers*, Bureau of Educational Research, Urbana, Illinois.

Gauvain, S., Wood, C. H., Walford, J., and Schilling, R. S. F. (1965), 'An experiment in postgraduate education to evaluate teaching and examination techniques', *J. med. Educ.*, vol. 40 (6), pp. 516–23.

Getzels, J. W., and Guba, E. G. (1957), 'Social behaviour and the administrative process', *Sch. Rev.*, vol. 65, pp. 423–41.

Goldfarb, W. (1955), 'Emotional and intellectual consequences of psychological deprivation in infancy: a re-evaluation', in Hoch, P. H., and Zubin, J. (eds.), *Psychopathology of Childhood*, Grune and Stratton.

Goldman, R. (1964), *Religious Thinking in Childhood and Adolescence*, Routledge and Kegan Paul.

Gottlieb, D. (1964), 'Teaching and students: the views of Negro and white teachers', *Sociol. Educ.*, vol. 37, pp. 345–53.

Gowan, J. C. (1955), 'Relation of the "K" scale of the M.M.P.I. to the teaching personality', *Calif. J. educ. Res.*, vol. 6, pp. 208–12.

Gross, N., and Herriot, R. E. (1965), *Staff Leadership in Public Schools*, Wiley.

Gross, N., Mason, W. S. and McEachern, A. W. (1958), *Explorations in Role Analysis: Studies of the School Superintendency Role* Wiley.

Guba, E. G., and Bidwell, C. E, (1957), *Administrative*

Relationships, Midwest Administration Center, University of Chicago.

Haddon, F. A., and Lytton, H. (1968), 'Teaching approach and the development of divergent thinking abilities in primary schools', *Brit. J. educ. Psychol.*, *vol.* 38 (2), pp. 171–9.

Half our Future (1963), *A Report of the Central Advisory Council for Education (England)*, H.M.S.O. (Newsom Report)

Hallworth, H. J. (1952), 'A study of group relationships among grammar school boys and girls between the ages of eleven and sixteen years', M.A. Thesis, University of London.

Hallworth, H. J. (1962), 'A teacher's perception of his pupils', *Educ. Rev.*, vol. 14, pp. 124–33.

Halpin, A. W. (1956), 'The leadership behaviour of school superintendents', *School-Community Development Study Monograph Series*, no. 4, Ohio State University.

Hannam, C., Smyth, P., and Stephenson, N. (1968), 'Bridging the class divide', *New Education*, January.

Hargreaves, D. H. (1967), *Social Relations in a Secondary School*, Routledge and Kegan Paul.

Harlow, H. F., and Harlow, M. K. (1962), 'Social deprivation in monkeys', *Sci. Amer.*, November.

Harvey, O. J., Prather, M. S., White, B. J., Alter, R. D., and Hoffmeister, J. K. (1966), 'Teachers' belief systems and pre-school atmosphere', *J. educ. Psychol.*, vol. 57 (6), pp. 373–81.

Harvey, O. J., Prather, M. S., White, B. J., and Hoffmeister, J. K. (1968), 'Teachers' beliefs, classroom atmospheres and student behaviour', *Amer. educ. Res. J.*, vol. 5 (2), pp. 151–66.

Hebb, D. O. (1955), 'Drives and the c.n.s. (conceptual nervous system)', *Psychol. Rev.*, vol. 62, pp. 243–54. Reprinted in Pribram, K. H. (ed,), *Brain and Behaviour 4: Adaptation*, Penguin Books, 1969.

Herriott, R. E., and St John, N. H. (1966), *Social Class and the Urban School*, Wiley.

Higher Education (1963), *The Report of the Committee appointed by the Prime Minister*, 1961–63, H.M.S.O. (Robbins Report)

Highfield, M. E., and Pinsent, A. (1952), *A Survey of Rewards and Punishments in Schools*, Newnes Educational.

Hovland, C. I., and Weiss, W. (1951), 'The influence of source credibility on communication effectiveness', *Public Opinion Quarterly*, vol. 15, pp. 635–50.

Hudson, L. (1967), *Contrary Imaginations*, Penguin Books.

Ishler, R. E. (1967), 'The effectiveness of feedback as a means of changing student teachers' verbal behaviour', *J. educ. Res.*, vol. 61(3), pp. 121–3.

Jackson, B. (1964), *Streaming: An Education System in Miniature*, Routledge and Kegan Paul.

Jackson, B., and Marsden, D. (1962), *Education and the Working Class*, Routledge and Kegan Paul.

Janis, I. L., and Feshbach, S. (1953), 'Effects of fear-arousing communications', *J. abnorm. soc. Psychol.*, vol. 48, pp. 78–92.

Jecker, J. D., Maccoby, H., and Breitrose, H. S. (1964), 'Teacher accuracy in assessing cognitive visual feedback', *J. appl. Psychol.*, vol. 48, pp. 393–7.

Jeffreys, M. V. C. (1961), *Revolution in Teacher Training*, Pitman.

Jenkins, D. H., and Lippitt, R. (1951), *Interpersonal Perceptions of Teachers, Students and Parents*, Division of Adult Education Services, National Education Association, Washington, D.C.

Johnson, M. E. B. (1966), 'Teachers' attitudes to educational research', *Educ. Res.*, vol. 9, pp. 74–9.

Joyce, B., Lamb, H., and Sibol, J. (1966), 'Conceptual development and information processing: a study of teachers', *J. educ. Res.*, vol. 59, pp. 219–22.

Joyce, C. R. B. ,and Weatherall, M. (1957), 'Controlled experiments in teaching', *Lancet*, 31 August, pp. 402–7.

Kahn, R. L. Wolfe, D. M., Quinn, R. P., Snock, J. D.,

and Rosenthal, R. A. (1964), *Organizational Stress: Studies in Role Conflict and Ambiguity*, Wiley.

Kelley, H. H. (1951), 'Communication in experimentally created hierarchies', *Human Relations*, vol. 4, pp. 39–56.

Kelman, H., and Hovland, C. (1953), '"Reinstatement" of the communicator in delayed measurement of opinion change', *J. abnorm. soc. Psychol.*, vol. 48, pp. 327–35.

Kennedy. W. A. ,and Willcutt, H. C. (1964), 'Praise and blame as incentives', *Psychol. Bull.*, vol. 62 (5), pp. 323–32.

Kounin, J. S., Friesen, W., and Norton, A. (1966), 'Managing emotionally disturbed children in regular classrooms', *J. educ. Psychol.*, vol. 57, pp. 1–13.

Kounin, J. S., and Gump, P. V. (1961), 'The comparative influence of punitive and non-punitive teachers upon childrens' concepts of school misconduct', *J. educ. Psychol.*, vol. 52, pp. 44–9.

Lantz, D. L. (1967), 'The relationship of university supervisors' and supervising teachers' ratings to observed student teachers', *Amer. educ. Res. J.*, vol. 4 (3), pp. 279–88.

Lippitt, R., and White, R. K. (1943), 'The "social climate" of children's groups', in Barker, R. G., Kounin, J. S., and Wright, H. F. (eds), *Child Behaviour and Development*, McGraw-Hill.

McCelland, D. C., Atkinson, J. W., Clark, R. A., and Lowell, E. L. (1953), *The Achievement Motive*, Appleton-Century-Crofts.

McIntyre, D., and Morrison, A. (1967), 'The educational opinions of teachers in training', *Brit. J. soc. clin. Psychol.*, vol. 6, pp. 32–7.

McIntyre, D., Morrison, A., and Sutherland, J. (1966), 'Social and educational variables relating to teachers' assessments of primary school pupils', *Brit. J. educ. Psychol.*, vol. 36, pp. 272–9.

McLeish, J. (1966), 'Student retention of lecture material', *Cambridge Institute of Education Bulletin*, vol. 3 (3), pp. 2–11.

Medley, D. M., and Mitzel, H. E. (1958), 'A technique for measuring classroom behaviour', *J. educ. Psychol.*, vol. 49, pp. 86–92.

Meux, M., and Smith, B. O. (1964), 'Logical dimensions of teaching behaviour', in Biddle, B. J., and Elena, W. J. (eds.), *Contemporary Research on Teacher Effectiveness*, Holt, Rinehart and Winston.

Milgram, S. (1964), 'Group pressure and action against a person', *J. abnorm. soc. Psychol.*, vol. 69 (2), pp. 137–43.

Miller, G., Galanter, E., and Pribram, K. (1960), *Plans and the Structure of Behavior*, Holt, Rinehart and Winston.

Mitzel, H. E. (1957), 'A behavioural approach to the assessment of teacher effectiveness', Division of Teacher Education, College of the City of New York, New York. (Mimeographed).

Morrison, A., and McIntyre, D. (1967), 'Changes in opinions about education during the first year of teaching', *Brit. J. soc. clin. Psychol.*, vol. 6, pp. 161–3.

Musgrove, F., and Taylor, P. H. (1965), 'Teachers' and parents' conceptions of the teacher's role', *Brit. J. educ. Psychol.*, vol. 35, pp. 171–8.

National Foundation for Educational Research (1967), 'The organization of junior schools and effects of streaming: a preliminary report', *Children and their Primary Schools*, A Report of the Central Advisory Council for Education (*England*), H.M.S.O., vol. 2, appendix 2.

Ojemann, R. H., and Wilkinson, F. R. (1939), 'The effect on pupil growth of an increase in teacher's understanding of pupil behaviour', *J. exp. Educ.*, vol. 8, pp. 143–7.

Oliver, R. A. C., and Butcher, H. J. (1962), 'Teachers' attitudes to education – the structure of educational attitudes', *Brit. J. soc. clin. Psychol.*, vol. 1, pp. 56–69.

Oliver, R. A. C., and Butcher, H. J. (1968), 'Teachers' attitudes to education', *Brit. J. educ. Psychol.*, vol. 38, pp. 38–44.

Olson, W. C. (1957), *Psychological Foundations of the Curriculum*, UNESCO Studies and Documents, no. 26, Paris.

Page, E. B. (1958), 'Teachers' comments and student performance', *J. educ. Psychol.*, vol. 49, pp. 173–81.

Parnes, S. J., and Brunelle, E. A. (1967), 'The literature
of creativity (Part I)', *J. creative Behav.*, vol. 1, pp. 52–
109.

Partridge, J. (1967), *Life in a Secondary Modern School*,
Penguin Books.

Peel, E. A. (1962) (Chairman), *Report of the Joint Working
Party of the British Psychological Society and the
Association of Teachers in Colleges and Departments of
Education on the Teaching of Educational Psychology in
Teacher Training*, British Psychological Society.

Piaget, J. (1952), *The Child's Conception of Number*,
Humanities Press.

Piaget, J., and Inhelder, B. (1965), *The Child's Conception
of Space*, Routledge and Kegan Paul.

Pickup, A. J., and Anthony, W. S. (1968), 'Teachers'
marks and pupils' expectations', *Brit. J. educ. Psychol.*,
vol. 38, pp. 302–9.

Polansky, L. (1954), 'Group social climate and the
teacher's supportiveness of group status systems', *J.
educ. Sociol.*, vol. 28, pp. 115–23.

Power, M. J., Alderson, M. R., Phillipson, C. M.,
Shoenberg, E., and Morris, J. N. (1967), 'Delinquency
and schools', *New Society*, no. 264, pp. 542–3.

Richardson, J. E. (1948), 'An investigation into group
methods of teaching English composition, with some
consideration of their effects on attainment and attitude
and a sociometric study of the two groups of children
involved', M.A. Thesis, University of London.

Robertson, J. D. C. (1957), 'An analysis of the views of
supervisors on the attributes of successful student
teachers', *Brit. J. educ. Psychol.*, vol. 27, pp. 115–26.

Rosenthal, R., and Jacobson, L. (1968), 'Teachers' expectations for the disadvantaged', *Sci. Amer.*, vol. 218 (4).

Rudd, W. G. A., and Wiseman, S. (1962), 'Sources of dissatisfaction among a group of teachers', *Brit. J. educ.
Psychol.*, vol. 32, pp. 275–91.

Runkel, P. J. (1958), 'A brief model for pupil–teacher interaction', in Gage, N. L. (ed.), *Handbook of Research on Teaching*, Rand McNally, pp. 126–7.

Runkel, P. J., and Damrin, D. E. (1961), 'Effects of training and anxiety upon teachers' preferences for information about students', *J. educ. Psychol.*, vol. 52 (5), pp. 254–61.

Ryans, D. G. (1960), *Characteristics of Teachers, Their Description, Comparison and Appraisal*, American Council on Education, Washington, D.C.

Ryans, D. (1963), 'Teacher behaviour theory and research: implications for teacher education', *J. teacher Educ.*, vol. 14, pp. 274–93.

Sarason, S. B., Davidson, K. S., and Blatt, B. (1962), *The Preparation of Teachers: An Unstudied Problem in Education*, Wiley.

Schueler, H., Gold, M. J., and Mitzel, H. E. (1962), *The Use of Television for Improving Teacher Training and for Improving Measures of Student-Teaching Performance. Phase 1: Improvement of Student Teaching*, The City University of New York.

Shipman, M. D. (1967), 'Theory and practice in the education of teachers', *Educ. Res.*, vol. 9, pp. 208–12.

Start, K. B. (1968), 'Rater-ratee personality in the assessment of teaching ability', *Brit. J. educ. Psychol.*, vol. 38, pp. 14–20.

Stevens, F. (1960), *The Living Tradition*, Hutchinson.

Stott, D. H. (1966), *Studies of Troublesome Children* Tavistock Publications.

Taylor, E. A. (1952), 'Some factors relating to social acceptance in eighth-grade classrooms', *J. educ. Psychol.*, vol. 43, pp. 257–72.

Taylor, P. H. (1962), 'Children's evaluations of the characteristics of a good teacher', *Brit. J. educ. Psychol.*, vol. 32, pp. 258–66.

Thelen, H. A. (1967), *Classroom Grouping for Teachability*, Wiley.

Torrance, E. P. (1960), *Education and Talent*, University of Minnesota Press.

Torrance, E. P. (1961), 'Primary creative thinking in the primary grades', *Elementary School J.*, vol. 62, pp. 34–41.

Tudhope, W. B. (1942), 'A study of the training college final teaching mark as a criterion of future success in the teaching profession', *Brit. J. educ. Psychol.*, vol. 12, pp. 167–71, and vol. 13, pp. 16–23.

Tudhope, W. B. (1944), 'Motives for the choice of the teaching profession by training college students', *Brit. J. educ. Psychol.*, vol. 14, pp. 129–41.

Turner, R. L. (1963), 'Task performance and teaching skill in the intermediate grades', in Silberman, H. F. (ed.), *A Symposium on Current Research on Classroom Behaviour of Teachers and its Implications for Teacher Education*, *J. Teacher Educ.*, vol. 14, September.

Wallach, M., and Kogan, N. (1965), *Modes of Thinking in Young Children*, Holt, Rinehart and Winston.

Warburton, F. W., Butcher, H. J., and Forrest, G. M. (1963), 'Predicting student performance in a university department of education', *Brit. J. educ. Psychol.*, vol. 33, pp. 68–79.

Washburne, C., and Heil, L. M. (1960), 'What characteristics of teachers affect children's growth?', *School Rev.*, vol. 68, pp. 420–28.

Williams, R. H. (1963), 'Professional studies in teacher training', *Educ. for Teaching*, vol. 61, pp. 29–33.

Willig, C. J. (1963), 'Social implications of streaming in the junior school', *Educ. Res.*, vol. 5, pp. 151–4.

Wilson, B. R. (1962), 'The teacher's role – a sociological analysis', *Brit. J. Sociol.*, vol. 13 (1), pp. 15–32.

Wiseman, S. (1964), *Education and Environment*, The University Press, Manchester.

Wiseman, S., and Start, K. B. (1965), 'A follow-up of teachers five years after completing their training', *Brit. J. educ. Psychol.*, vol. 35, pp. 342–61.

Withall, J. (1951), 'The development of the climate index', *J. educ. Res.*, vol. 45, pp. 93–100.

Withall, J. (1956), 'An objective measure of a teacher's

classroom interactions', *J. educ. Res.*, vol. 47, pp. 203–12.

Wright, B. D., and Tuska, S. A. (1966), *From Dream to Life in the Psychology of Becoming a Teacher: Student and First Year Teachers' Attitudes towards Self and Others*, U.S. Department of Health, Education and Welfare, Office of Education, Co-operative Research Project no. 1503, University of Chicago.

Wright, E. M. J. (1959), 'Development of an instrument for studying verbal behaviours in a secondary school mathematics classroom', *J. exp. Educ.*, vol. 28, pp. 103–21.

Yates, A. (1966), *Grouping in Education*, UNESCO Institute for Education, Hamburg.

Index

Index

Abstractness–concreteness
 137–8
Achievement
 assessment of scholastic
  19–21, 169–70, 172–3
 motivation 126–9
 of student teachers 66–7
Affiliation 122–6, 163–4
Altman, E. 49
American Educational
 Research Association 17
Anastasiow, N. J. 179
Anderson, R. C. 135
Anthony, W. S. 178
Argyle, M. 24, 163
Asch, S. 124, 174
Ashley, B. 45, 49
Assessment 169–82
 of pupils' achievements
  19–21
 of students' teaching 53
Attention 160, 182
Attitudes
 influencing pupils' 164–8
 parents', to education
  76–81, 128–9
 pupils', to teachers 104
 pupils', to teaching as a
  career 46
 students', to college
  courses 64–6
 teachers'
 and social class background
  of schools 99
 associated with streaming
  102
 in grammar schools
  94–6
 in secondary modern

 schools 96–8
 to educational issues 23,
  46, 68–72, 90–91
 to parents 80
 to pupils 179
 to research 82–3
Audiovisual systems 32
Authoritarian teaching 133,
 145

Bach, J. O. 54
Bandura, A. 143
Becker, H. S. 99, 100
Bellak, A. A. 32
Bernstein, B. 156
Biddle, B. J. 39, 79
Bidwell, C. E. 88
Blatt, B. 61
Bloom, B. S. 18
Blyth, W. A. L. 118, 175
Bogen, I. 118
Bonney, M. 176
Bovard, E. W. 117
Bruckman, I. R. 128
Brunelle, E. A. 136
Bruner, J. S. 59, 174
Bryan, J. H. 143
Butcher, H. J. 23, 54, 69, 97

Callis, R. 23, 69
Categories of teacher
 behaviour 29–31
Childhood experiences of
 teachers 47–8
Child-rearing practices 128
Children and Their Primary
 Schools 77, 81, 99, 128,
 140
Clark, R. P. 65

Clegg, A. B. 146, 148
Cognitive development
  154–5
Cohen, H. 45, 49
Cohen, L. 70, 71, 78
Colleges of education
  goals of 56–7
  qualifications for entry 43
  relations of staff with
    serving teachers 81
  staff and teaching methods
    63–4
  student-staff ratios 63
  students' attitudes to
    courses in 64–6
Collins, M. 67
Commitment 167
Competition 117, 125
Communication
  and group cohesiveness 116
  in the classroom 151–68
  in committees 107
  within schools 85–6
  parent–teacher 77–81
Conflict among teachers
  91–3
  with team teaching 107
Conformity 46–7, 91, 124
Cook, W. W. 23
Co-operation 117, 125
Cornwell, J 55
Craig, H. 97, 98
Creativity 134–6
Credibility 167
Crutchfield, R. S. 135
Cues 170–78

Damrin, D. E. 184
Davidson, K. S. 61
Delinquency 116, 146–7
Democratic teaching 133
Deutsch, M. 117, 125
Dickson, G. 66, 69
Dissatisfaction of
  teachers 89–90
Dominance 122–6, 163–4

Douglas, J. W. B. 76

Educational background of
  teachers 42
Educational objectives
  18–19
Effectiveness of teachers 14, 16
  criteria for 15, 16–24, 52
Entwhistle, N. J. 128
Evans, D. 127
Evans, K. M. 46, 69, 108
Expectations
  pupils', of teachers 109–11
  teachers', of pupils 179–82
Eye contact 163

Feedback 24–5, 178
Feshbach, S. 166
Festinger, L. 131
Finlayson, D. S. 70, 71
Flanders, N. A. 29, 62, 152
Flavell, J. H. 131
Forrest, G. M. 54
Friesen, W. 144

Gage, N. L. 177, 178, 183
Gauvain, S. 161
Getzels, J. W. 87, 109
Goldfarb, W. 123
Goldman, R. 155
Gottlieb, D. 179
Gowan, J. C. 46
Graduate teachers 43, 67
Grammar schools 94–6
Gross, N. 39, 86
Grouping of pupils 101,
  111–13, 125–6, 158–61
Guba, E. G. 87, 88
Gump, P. V. 143

Haddon, F. A. 135
Half our Future, 96, 99
Hallworth, H. J. 125, 170
Halpin, A. W. 87, 88
Hannam, C. 157
Hargreaves, D. H. 89, 97,
  103, 114

Harlow, H. F. 123
Harlow, M. K. 123
Harvey, O. J. 23, 137, 138
Headmasters 84–8
  ratings of teachers by 53,
  54
Hebb, D. O. 131
Heil, L. M. 138
Herriott, R. E. 86, 100
Higher Education, 43, 44, 63
Highfield, M. E. 139–40
Hovland, C. 167
Hudson, L. 134

Impression formation 174
Indirect–direct teacher
  influence 31, 153
Influencing pupils'
  attitudes 164–8
Information
  effects of increasing 176–8
  processing of 169–70
Inhelder, B. 155
Inspectors 82
Intelligence
  and achievement motivation
  128
  growth of 131
  of teachers 47
Interaction
  teacher–pupil 24–34, 53
  analysis of 29–31, 62
Intrinsic motivation 129–32
Ishler, R. E. 183

Jackson, B. 77, 102
Jacobson, L. 180
Janis, I. L. 166
Jecker, J. D. 183
Jeffreys, M. V. C. 57
Jenkins, D. H. 39, 79
Johnson, M. E. B. 82, 83
Joyce, B. 138
Joyce, C. R. B. 161

Kahn, R. L. 36

Kelley, H. H. 86, 112
Kelman, H. 167
Kennedy, W. A. 141
Kogan, N. 134
Kounin, J. S. 32, 143,
  144

Laboratory research 14, 32,
  34, 91
Lamb, H. 138
Language, modes of, in the
  classroom 155–7
Lantz, D. L. 53
Leadership
  professional 87–8
  training in 95
Lectures 58, 64, 161–2
Leeds, C. H. 23
Lewin, K. 133
Lippitt, R. 39, 79, 133, 143,
  145
Logical behaviour of
  teachers 33, 153–5
Lytton, H. 135

McClelland, D. C. 127
McIntyre, D. 46, 69, 70,
  99, 168, 171
McLeish, J. 161
Maladjustment 148–9
Manchester Opinion Scales
  on Education 23, 69, 70
Marking by teachers 178
Marsden, D. 77
Maternal deprivation 123
Mature students 49
Medley, D. M. 29
Methods lectures 58–9
Meux, M. 154
Micro-teaching 62
Milgram, S. 124
Miller, G. 131
Minnesota Multiphasic
  Personality Inventory
  46, 70

Minnesota Teacher Attitude
  Inventory 23, 68, 69
Mitzel, H. E. 16, 29
Model
  for pupil–teacher
    interaction 25–6
  for study of roles in
    organizations 36–9
  of skilled performances 24
  of teacher effectiveness 15
Morrison, A. 46, 69, 70,
  168, 171
Motives
  classification of 121
  for becoming teachers 43,
    48–50
Motivation
  achievement 126–9
  intrinsic 129–32
  social 122–9
Musgrove, F. 79, 80, 92,
  93, 97

National Foundation for
  Educational Research
  102
Nisbet, J. D. 65
Non-verbal behaviour 162–4
Norms for teacher behaviour
  parents' 79
  pupils' 108–9
  teachers' 79–80
Norton, A. 144

Obedience 124
Observation of classroom
  behaviour 22, 27–33, 53,
  60, 169
Observation Schedule and
  Record (OSCAR) 29
Ojemann, R. H. 176
Oliver, R. A. C. 23, 69, 97
Olson, W. C. 158
Organization

classroom 111–13, 125–6,
  157–61
school 85–9, 101–8

Page, E. B. 178
Parent–teacher
  relationships 76–81
Parnes, S. J. 136
Partridge, J. 85, 90
Peaker, G. F. 128
Peel, E. A. 57
Peers 103, 123, 124, 143,
  167, 175, 183
Perception
  of headmasters' behaviour
    88
  of norms and expectations
    36–9, 79–80
  of pupils' characteristics
    170–71
  of pupils' understanding
    183
Permissiveness 145
Personality characteristics
  of teachers 14, 16, 22–4,
    45–7
  of teachers and pupils
    137–9
  and persuasion 168
Piaget, J. 131, 154–5
Pickup, A. J. 178
Pinsent, A. 139–40
Polansky, L. 118
Power, M. J. 146
Practice teaching 59–63
Praise, effects of 141
Prediction of teaching
  ability 54–6
Professional education of
  teachers 56–72
Progressiveness 69, 72, 134
Psychology in teacher
  education 57–8
Punishment
  corporal 140–41, 147
  effects of 141–3

Rankin, E. F.   79
Ratings
  of pupils   170–72
  of teachers   21–2, 28, 52–3
Relations between teachers
    and pupils   108–18
  effects of streaming on
    103–5
  effects of team teaching
    on   108
Reliability
  of observation of classroom
    behaviour   29
  of ratings   22
  of reports of headmasters'
    behaviour   88
Richardson, J. E.   125
Robertson, J. D. C.   52
Role of the teacher   34–40,
  75, 106
Rosencranz, H. A.   79
Rosenthal, R.   180
Rudd, W. G. A.   89, 90
Runkel, P. J.   25, 184
Ryans, D. G.   28, 133, 134,
  169

St John, N. H.   100
Sanctions
  in the classroom   139–43
  on school superintendents
    40
Sarason, S. B.   61
Schueler, H.   68
Secondary modern schools
  96–8
Selection of teachers   42,
  51–6
Sensory deprivation   130
Sex of teachers   45, 51
Shipman, M. D.   71
Sibol, J.   138
Skills, model for   24
Skills, teaching   27, 41,
  65–6, 157, 162
  assessment   173, 175

class management   65, 132,
  144, 160
integration of verbal and
  non-verbal   163
training in   58, 61–3, 66–8,
  72, 74, 182–5
Slatter, R.   45, 49
Smith, B. O.   154
Social background
  of teachers   44
  of schools   99–101
Social groups
  among teachers   89–90
  among pupils   113–18,
    123–5
Social structure of the
  classroom group   111–18,
  175
Sociometric tests   55, 114–5,
  183
Start, K. B.   53, 56
Stereotypes   98, 104, 108–9,
  171
Stevens, F.   94, 96
Stott, D. H.   147
Streaming   101–5
Styles of teaching   133–6
Supervisors   52–5, 60–61, 68
Sutherland, J.   171

Taylor, E. A.   117
Taylor, P. H.   79, 80, 92,
  93, 97, 109
Teacher Characteristics
  Schedule 28
Teachers' comments   178
Teaching marks   52–4
Team teaching   105–8
Thelen, H. A.   139
Torrance, E. P.   134, 135
Training, effects of
  on attitudes   68–72
  on classroom behaviour   68
  on skills and knowledge
    66–8
Troublesome pupils   143–9

Tudhope, W. B. 49, 55
Turner, R. L. 67
Tuska, S. A. 48
Tutorials 64, 161–2

University Grants Committee
63

Values, teachers' 46
Verbal behaviour, patterns
of 152–3

Wallach, M. 134
Walters, R. H. 143
Warburton, F. W. 15, 54

Washburne, C. 138
Weatherall, M. 161
Weiss, W. 167
White, R. K. 133, 143, 145
Wilkinson, F. R. 176
Willcutt, H. C. 141
Williams, R. H. 64
Willig, C. J. 102
Wilson, B. R. 39
Wiseman, S. 16, 56, 89, 90,
128, 134, 137, 147
Withall, J. 160, 183
Wright, B. D. 48
Wright, E. M. J. 33

Yates, A. 101